Volume 8 Issue 1
The Healing Issue
www.inspiritmagazine.com

Editor's Note

One of my favourite quotes is "Sometimes when things seem like they are falling apart, they may actually be falling into place" - Author Unknown.

Certainly when creating this issue of inSpirit Magazine, it has felt this way as it was coming together.

Healing energy, and what it brings to your life, has a way of breaking things down so we can start anew and put ourselves and our lives back together in a way that serves our soul in a whole new and more desirable way.

As you read through this Healing edition of inSpirit, we are sure you will find many moments of inspiration that will aid in letting go and starting fresh, whether it is simply a matter of letting go of 2014 and moving full force into 2015, or something far deeper within your Soul's journey. Healing is an ongoing process for us all and much of this issue is designed to support you during these times.

Spirit very specifically asked me to feature a sound healer in this issue, so we feel honoured to have Laura Naomi speak with Medicine Man Rusty Baldeagle Myers, about how music and shamanism combine beautifully for healing.

This issue we farewell Natasha Heard, this being her last article for us. We thank Natasha for her energy, enthusiasm and contributions over the last couple of years. We have been blessed to have you and are wishing you much love for all your future endeavours. As one door closes another opens, as we welcome Amanda Rousetty, 2013 IPA Psychic of the Year, on board as a regular contributor. Amanda's warmth and heartfelt insights will be a welcome addition to the pages of inSpirit.

Lastly, there is a little excitement here at inSpirit HQ. We are now available on your mobile devices. That's right, you can now read your copy of inSpirit on your Android reader, your Apple iPad or iPhone. How exciting! Visit iTunes or the Google play store and search inSpirit Magazine and Voila! What a great start to 2015 for us!

With love & gratitude, Kerrie

In This Issue

16 Year of the Wood Sheep

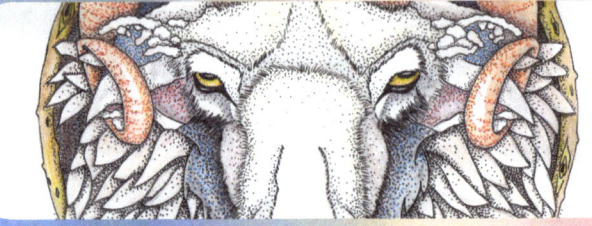

3   Dot by Tiny Dot
4   2015 - A Soul Conversation
6   The Sounds of Earth
8   The Miracle of Harry
9   Self Healing with Regression
10 Healing
12 Faery Reiki
14 Love Never Dies
16 Year of the Wood Sheep
18 Divine Healing through Dreaming
20 The Healer
22 Healing Your Soul in a Chaotic World
23 Children and Healing with Angels
24 A Little Heaing Goes a Long Way
26 A Blessing in Disguise
28 Playful Healing
30 Shell Vibrations

Regular Columns

13 Crystal Q & A
17 Cosmic Codes
21 For the Love of Angels
32 inSpirit Reviews
33 inSpirit Directory

THE TEAM

MANAGING EDITOR Kerrie Wearing

CREATIVE TEAM Kerrie Wearing, Nicolle Poll, Alex Cayas, Therese Chesworth and Nicola McIntosh

EDITOR Nicolle Poll, Therese Chesworth

REGULAR CONTRIBUTORS Kerrie Wearing, Nicolle Poll, Nicola McIntosh, Susanne Hartas, Jude Downes, Gem Green, Meadow Linn, Alex Cayas, Natasha Heard, Laura Naomi, Kye Crow, Reilly McCarron, Rita Maher, Amanda Coppa, Toni Reilly

GUEST CONTRIBUTORS Sue Bishop, Laura Bowen, Nathan Ho

GRAPHIC DESIGN Kerrie Wearing, Nicola McIntosh

COVER ARTWORK Nicolle Poll

6

8

14

Produced by Kerrie Wearing and inSpirit Publishing, inSpirit Magazine is designed to provide a respectful forum for like-minded souls to share in a community which aims to provide informative views, opinions and education regarding the experience of living with Spirit. Disclaimer: While every care has been taken to provide the reader with accurate, inSpiring and thought-provoking information, the Publishers take no responsibility for the accuracy of information and views expressed by the Contributors. The views and opinions expressed by contributors are not necessarily shared by the Editor Publishers.

Dot by Tiny Dot

A Journey to Healing

This month's guest contributor Laura Bowen shares her very personal story of healing after post natal depression.

Just over 18 months ago, I found myself in a state of depression after the birth of my fifth child. I felt lost, confused, overwhelmed, exhausted and not quite sure what to do about it.

I decided I needed to do something for my children, for my partner, but most importantly for myself. I needed to rediscover who I was, to make time for myself. I needed to laugh, to create, to remember and share my story and my experiences. I needed to reintroduce myself to the woman I had become. Little did I know that by making that decision to find myself, I would also find an incredible healing for myself and my little tribe.

When my first baby was born, I embraced my new-found motherhood with everything I had and continued to as the years passed and another 4 children were birthed by me.

Last year I learned that to put others' needs ahead of your own does not work. In the midst of chaos I heard the whispers of spirit calling to me and encouraging me to step outside, to stand bare foot on the rich earth.

I listened to my soul and the voices of my ancestors as they travelled on the wind and vibrated up from below my feet. I knew that I was here for a reason, to accomplish more that I had and I decided to find my path. I had no idea what that path would be or where it would take me.

I have always felt a strong connection to the land I live on. My daily ritual is watching the coming and going of the natural wildlife, the dawning of the sun and the last rays on the horizon in the evenings. This connection to place has always helped me feel grounded. It reminds me that I am just one small part of the whole and that there is much to learn from nature in all its beauty and vulnerability.

During a barefoot walk through the bush around my home I discovered a magpie feather. It inspired me, so I took it home. The next day I went out and bought paints and canvas. That night I used the feather to dot a painting of an animal that has always frequented my home. The goanna - which for me represents self-preservation and the ability to overcome adversity.

As I dotted, each tiny dot represented a tiny moment immortalized forever in a microcosm of colour. The dots together represented tiny thoughts, mind moments of vulnerability, knowledge, sadness, hopelessness and pride.

When the painting was completed I looked at the story I had shared with all those tiny dots and yearned to tell another, to capture each little mind bubble and transfer its emotion in colour to an artwork that would tell a story.

Each day I painted the animal and insect messengers from around my home. Sometimes tears would fall and I would not know why, but each day I would learn a little more about who I was and was a little more sure about what it was I was here to do.

I blogged online throughout my "journey back to me" through my art to my handful of followers I had never met from different parts of the world. I shared the moments of achievement along with the moments of overwhelming rawness. I found that by creating a space to share my personal journey, my story that only I can tell, I was able to receive support and encouragement, but more importantly I was creating a space where others could be real and share their personal experiences as well.

I know we often say that each person has a story. But I had never really understood how important and how healing it is to allow ourselves and others the opportunity share it; to become the storyteller of the story that is our own journey, our life experience.

With each new dotted artwork I create, I see in it so many moments of time spent just for me doing something I enjoy, my own personal form of mediation. My journey to healing taught me the importance of honoring myself and following my dreams as well as engaging in real conversation where you not only speak but actively listen too, because everyone has their own story to tell.

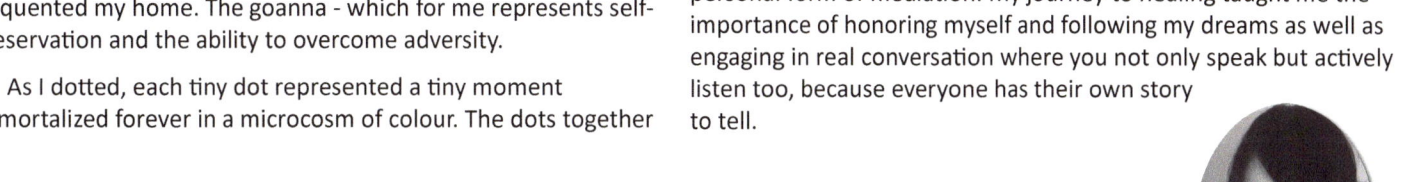

Laura Bowen is an Aboriginal Artist and Author, she is the creator of the "Dreamtime Reading Cards" published by Rockpool Publishing and due for release in February 2015. www.laurabowen.com.au

2015 - A Soul Conversation

Kerrie Wearing, our managing editor intuitively reviews 2015 to see what the universal energies have install for us next year, giving you insight designed to help you power through 2015 with heightened awareness.

To begin intuitively connecting with 2015, I began by using my Daily Soul Conversation insight cards which are ideal to give you an insight into the creative and spiritual energies supporting us all for next year. I then followed this with drawing one of my Spirit Guide Wisdom insight cards for each month of the year and delving intuitively a little to see what it holds for you.

As I shuffled the Soul Conversation card, not one but two cards jumped out together, making themselves known for you.

Daily Soul Conversation card 1: "Please reveal to me, what it is that my Spirit needs today...."

Being guided by Spirit is becoming more and more prominent across the collective consciousness, and there is a strong sense the flow will enhance for you the more you trust. This is a year to keep a handle on allowing Spirit to guide you. These energies are really heightened throughout 2015 with increasing synchronicity.

You may find that what may feel like everything falling apart is really Spirit's guiding hand helping you to let go of what does not serve you, so you can create anew. Allow it to be and use prayer to ease any resistance.

Many of you will experience more of this letting go, and some of you will have a sense of rising from the ashes, like you've been here before and only now can see the purpose behind all you've been through to recognize your truth and who you need to be to effect more positive and desirable outcomes.

Get this right and your struggles diminish as you feel the flow beneath you like a gentle rolling river.

Daily Soul Conversation card 2: "To be humble is to not know you are. I truly appreciate acting with humbleness in all that I do today."

Any challenges that do present this year are best approached with humbleness. Take your time to step back first before reacting and see your way to moving through your challenges with gentleness and humbleness. This response will see the ebb and flow of life move along more graciously.

Not every challenge that presents is there for your learning. Some have you simply being the mirror, and the best and most impactful mirror is one that stands strong in truth, with awareness and humbleness - not one that simply reflects.

Aligning the energies of these two areas of Soul awareness by more consciously following the guidance of your Divine Spirit, while living and expanding humbleness, will see you walk graciously throughout 2015.

January - Buffalo and Universal Abundance

We start the year with a feeling of tranquillity, optimism and looking forward with new hope. Eradicate any doubt or pessimism by focusing your choices and requests of the Universe. Keep it simple and the rewards will follow.

Release and relax the purse strings to see money flow. Holding tight here at this time will see an energy of fear created, repelling any flow coming to you. It is a good time to revitalize your health regime, as it is for moving into new awareness with any new forms of learning and personal/spiritual growth and development.

February - Leprechaun, The Mischief Maker

This month you need to be aware of where you may get in your own way. Watch out for becoming easily distracted from what's important to you and losing focus from any goals you may have set yourself.

With any job or career opportunities that present this month, be sure to ask yourself if they are aligned with your long term vision. Will they support what it is you are working towards? If not, it is okay to say no, for they may have you distracted and veering along an unnecessary detour.

March - Dog and Loyalty

Friendships and relationships come to the fore this month. Some of you will be creating new partnerships, while others will be letting go and clearing way for new friendships which are more aligned with who you have become. It is a time for new interests, new parties, so get out and have some fun this month.

April - Angel and Protection

Alarm bells right around this month. It is a month to be extra cautious with your safety. Heightened awareness and vigilance is called for as the world spins from some catastrophic events, which feel war related. Be mindful of offering the world healing and helping the global energies come back into balance by being in balance yourself and sharing this with the world around you. Remember in Oneness, we are.

May - Egyptian and Worldly Abundance

If you have been knuckling down and applying yourself to taking action, this month should see some great results for you as new paths unfold. There is an increase in abundance, including your finances. Job promotions are on the horizon as people are becoming aware of your talents, and you begin to be recognized for all that you do.

June - Owl and All Seeing Wisdom

Shelter from the storm - new circumstances can unhinge things a little as those around you try to adjust. Patience and understanding will help ease any unsettledness at this time.

It is a time to see beyond what's being presented at face value to ease yourself through any troubled water. Be cautious of new opportunities, as they may not be all they are cracked up to be. Listen to any heightened intuition this month.

July - The Old Man and Your Higher Self

Celebrate! The hard work is paying off as from here things get, and flow, a little easier. Your intuitive voice is strong and will guide your choices, providing you with clarity as you find yourself presented with several decision to make this month - choices which affect your home and your lifestyle. Again, listen to that intuitive voice. It is your Higher Self expressing itself, and it knows all and sees the way forward clearly. Do not be afraid to step into unknown territory for the rewards can be great.

August - Eagle and New Understandings

This month it will be easy to feel overwhelmed as it feels like every man and his dog will want a piece of you. You could find yourself feeling like you are being pulled in every direction, so try to stay focused on what is important for you.

New awareness, new exposure, new surroundings all feature, as Eagle takes you places you haven't been before as travel takes a focus. Explore to your heart's content as you travel and begin to lay new foundations for the year ahead. You'll also be expanding your financial prospects at this time as well.

September - Deer and the Art of Gentleness

Proceed with gentleness this month. Watch and think before you respond or act, as situations can all too easily erupt and turn negative, causing hurt to all involved.

Where you are seeing the presence of constant challenges, the tides turned, or where you begin to feel as if you are up against it, look more closely in this area of your life, as these are telling signs that it is time to let go and close that door. 'Let go' would be a great keyword phrase for this month.

October - Dragon and Intuitive Guidance

Challenges present this month where you can be in two minds and not wanting to let go, holding on to what you have always known. Trust in Dragon and your intuition. You may not see the outcome, but trust that all will be revealed in time.

Be clear as to whether it is obligation that is holding you back from letting go.

November - Dove and Peace

Winding down - the past couple of months have weighed heavy, though now you are getting through it. Different challenges for people, be it personal or professional, this month. You will start to see the light and a calmness begins to kick in. Just keep putting one foot in front of the other.

December - The Light of Love and Enlightenment

Hark! The Herald Angels sing as the storm passes and new beginnings await. It has been a challenging last three months with this month,

December, seeing an end to it. So having weathered that storm, relax, enjoy the coming festive season and breathe in the new energy that is flowing in.

Kerrie Wearing is an internationally recognised Soul Coach and Medium, specialising in coaching and mentoring people to connect with their unique Soul Purpose. She is the author of A New Kind of Normal; Unlock the Medium Within, managing editor of inSpirit Magazine and director of inSpirit Publishing. Website: www.kerriewearing.com

THE SOUNDS OF EARTH

LAURA NAOMI EXPLORES THE SHAMANIC PRACTICE OF MUSIC AND ITS HEALING EFFECTS WITH THIS THERAPEUTIC INTERVIEW OF MEDICINE MAN RUSTY BALDEAGLE MYERS

When I had the great honour of interviewing medicine man Rusty Baldeagle Myers, I felt humbled. He resonates a gentle peace and a deeply honest energy, and I know in these moments it is a time to listen carefully. Baldeagle is also a caretaker of sacred land in the United States. For over 30 years he's been practicing as a medicine man involved with Hopi and Lakota elders and influential in community building around the world.

I feel a deep wisdom and although his answers to my questions are short, they are to the point and the energy is beautiful. As a singer and a classical musician, music has been part of my creative expression all of my life. It has touched me in many significant ways - great spiritual moments have been accessed through music, song and sound. I feel passionate hearing about how it has stirred spirit in another, in an area of life I feel so drawn to. For example, when I experience the spirit of song in my body I cannot help but move to the rhythm of its energy - it emerges like the wind or the flames of fire, and continues flowing until a calm space follows, integrating the dance.

Music and sound are the essence of some shamanic healings. To me even silence is music, and to be in tune with the song of the moment and what is required is the key.

Baldeagle uses several Native American and Shamanic instruments; the rattle, drum and flute along with singing bowls and his voice. *"Sound is heard through the auditory senses but is also heard through the body as vibrations, which carries spiritual awakenings and awareness."* Baldeagle predominantly uses the Native American flute in his healings and readings. *"I was given a Native American flute not knowing I could play and after a few moments I began to make music with the flute. Not necessarily music that I was familiar with but I soon found out it was similar to many Native American flute melodies. I rarely play the same melody the same way"* he adds.

Music unleashes stagnant and blocked energy - releasing, moving and giving it the opportunity to then be restored and replenished. For example, in my sacred space I have a singing bowl for each chakra to play the specific tone in order to help with clearing and healing. Sound is used for many different reasons in relationship to healing and energy - it is particularly powerful in clearing space.

"I have used the flute in healings in regard to shamanic readings. I use the flute as a form of prayer to begin the reading. I also use the flute in regards to Native American sweat lodges and when I do a clearing or healing for an individual" says Baldeagle. He also elaborates about the shamanic drum after asking what he feels is a powerful musical instrument to shift energy. *"The Native American drum is powerful because it evokes spiritual clarity through its rhythm, vibration and sound. It's also powerful because of its ability to cut through denial, barriers and misunderstandings."*

On a personal note, the voice has been quite powerful in healing, clearing and preparing space. I did not recognise this until a medicine woman came into my life as a teenager. I was incredibly shy and she kept encouraging me to sing, usually accompanying her. One evening she offered the space for me to sing while she played the guitar. I felt something haunting rise from within me and it sounded like the voice of spirit flowing rather than my own. In this moment and moments hereafter, I feel both present in my body yet outside myself at the same time. It was the song of spirit and at this time of recognition, I felt so connected - a part of the Universe, yet feeling my humanness. The medicine woman had seen this song inside me and I feel her recognition created healing for me to perhaps initiate the same in others.

I've seen the power in sound healing and the energy that can be channeled and for me it is important to hold a deep respect for the songs that are handed to us to sing as medicine men or women.

"If someone is wanting to play an instrument or use sound in shamanic healings/ceremonies, they need to take it seriously. In other words, this person needs to be clear and sure that they are feeling called as a healer or to a shamanic life-journey." Baldeagle began to speak about how healing and significant a song and music can be with humanity. It is a universal language, much like love. We all have a connection to sound, in its various melodies and expressions. Following is a powerful representation of such, spoken in a traditional story-telling manner by Baldeagle.

"The Hopi people, for possibly thousands of years, have been waiting to hear the Purification Song. It became known through vision that a Hopi holy man called Titus was to sing the song during the Time of Purification. The first sign of the beginning of the Time of Purification was the Gourd of Ashes (The atomic bombing of Hiroshima, Japan) in 1945. Some 49 years later, Titus began to sing the song during a sacred ceremony in Hotavilla, Hopi, USA. The other elders during the ceremony asked him to stop because they felt he was singing the song before its time."

Baldeagle had a dream.

"He went underground way below the roots. When he got down there, there were many people. Most he didn't know. Off to the left in a dark place a very old man began to sing. Baldeagle got frightened and grabbed for the roots and began to pull himself up. As he got close to the surface he stopped and realised he needed to go back and retrieve the song.

Through vision and people's help Baldeagle went to Titus and sang the song. Titus was pleased and Baldealge has been singing the Song of Purification around the world since."

We are still in the time of purification and the song is about healing the pain that humans carry.

There are many ways to shift pain in the form of sound - in the shamanic culture sound healing is a strong aspect of doing so. Part of the songs of spirit involves channeling energy; from a particular source (e.g. the energy of an animal or nature) or Universal energy. It is powerful because it also involves storytelling, inspiration, specific sounds and melodies that carry messages intended to awaken and heal. There is a wood-turner in the United Kingdom who creates sound bowls, strung with pentatonic strings tuned to the pentatonic scale which therapists use for healing. Another healer uses his voice toning and was trained by Monks. Whatever mode of music moves you to the core and fires your spirit, this is the song of you, the sound of the Universe.

"It's not about what you know or don't know. It's not about what you will learn or not learn. It is about trust, it is about faith. One must always follow the call, never believe they're doing it, have no attachment to outcome and seek no return." – Rusty Baldeagle Myers

Aho.

Rusty Baldeagle Myers – Contact details:
Ph: +1 (785) 760-2714,
email: rmyers@ix.netcom.com

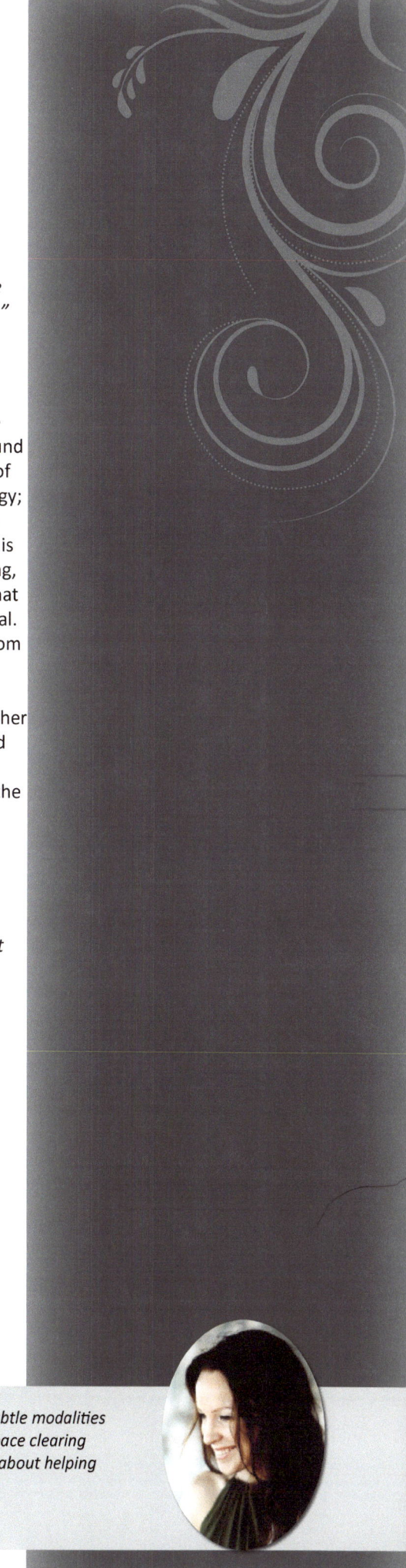

Laura Naomi specialises in increasing awareness around energy and how we relate through the more subtle modalities of communication. She uses a blend of unique modalities - Zen practices, Shamanism, energy healing, space clearing and psychic and emotional counselling. She guides individuals, groups and businesses and is passionate about helping others harness their innate magic to expand their quiet knowing and wisdom

Website: www.laura-naomi.com Phone: +1 (785) 813-8005

The Miracle of Harry

The love between Kye and Harry shows us all, that anything is possible.

by Kye Crowe

One day a very special chicken came into my life. She had barely a feather on her body, had never been loved or looked after, and her name was Harry.

I absolutely adored her. We had many chickens at the time, yet Harry stood out, and you could tell the love we shared was mutual; she always ran up to greet me and followed me everywhere like a little dog.

We hadn't had her very long when one morning I went down to feed my chickens and I was devastated to find her lying on the ground looking really miserable. When I picked her up I noticed a lump on her rear and I knew if we wanted to save her we had to act fast. I rang our local vet and told him what had happened and the beautiful man replied *"Oh the poor love, she must be in pain, bring her in immediately."*

When later he examined her he told us that it looked as if she had a cyst on her uterus and in his experience he had never seen a chicken recover from this condition. He gently offered to put her down. I found myself in such a dilemma. Of course I didn't want to prolong her suffering. I liked to think I believed in miracles, yet I was full of fear. What if she didn't recover? I couldn't face the prospect of prolonging her pain and then having to put her down myself. I wavered in uncertainty until I saw the look in Harry's eyes. She was looking directly at me with so much trust and love and I knew exactly what I had to do.

I thanked the vet for his kindness, gathered Harry into my arms and told him I was taking my little chook home.

Every day after, my partner Gill and I would sit with Harry and give her hands-on healing. It would have been easy to focus on what was wrong and problems that on the surface seemed insurmountable, but I knew the most potent way to heal was to hold a vision of Harry shining with health, radiant and well, and that's what we did.

The following morning I was relieved to see Harry looking so much brighter. Within a day or two she was up and walking about and everyday her painful lump got smaller and smaller, until two weeks later it had completely disappeared. Our little chicken was blossoming in health and all her feathers were beginning to grow!

Some of my most powerful teachers have come from the animal realms and I intuitively knew that Harry had come simply to teach me about the power of love.

It was so easy to be present in love with Harry. My heart opened every time I saw her and in this divine space the healing energy had flowed. The beautiful connection we shared showed me what was possible, but when I'm struggling to find that space now, I do something I love. I take a candlelit bath, create a sacred ritual, sit under a huge old tree or light some candles and incense and relax to some uplifting and inspirational music.

If fears come up, I imagine them floating away like balloons, getting smaller and smaller as they drift away up into the sky until they are gone.

Thanks to Harry I no longer believe in limitations. Anything is possible if we believe it is so. The source of love flows from within us and that's why it's essential to nurture and honour ourselves. The loving energy we give ourselves feeds and nourishes the flow of love in our lives. This is the source of all healing and the sacred space in which anything is possible and miracles can occur.

Harry lived a long and healthy life and ended her physical journey a much-loved chook, but our connection was of the heart and I still feel her presence around me. Some days when I'm sitting at the computer too long or I'm putting my needs to one side, she will pop up and ask me what I am choosing today.

Is it the miracles or the mundane?

For in every moment we have a choice and in our modern busy lives it's so easy to forget that nothing sacred grows in stress. So I turn off my computer, thank my little chook; drink a glass of water and head outside for a walk!

Kye Crow is the Creatress of Wunjo Crow, a range of Goddess clothing that's sprinkled with love and sewn with magic. Kye and her partner Gill live with over a 100 rescued animals and teach Sacred Journeys into the Animal Realms, the power of Love and how to live on planet earth as a sensitive. **Contact Kye at:** Web: www.camelcampsanctuary.com Facebook: www.facebook.com/Wunjocrow

Self Healing with Regression

TONI REILLY explores the use of Past Life Regression and its capabilities for self healing.

Exploring your past life, between life and earlier in current life memories, is not about dredging up the past. They hold profound knowledge and core experiences to improve current life and assist you to live your life to the fullest and most rewarding extent possible.

Experiencing past lives, earlier in current life or soul life memories can bring clarity around current behaviours, fears, phobias and patterns in relationships. It helps identify the source of these feelings and fears. Understanding an event, which created a fear, phobia, or a recurring dream, can remove the current symptoms and free you to live a happy, fulfilled life.

It is possible to relieve and heal physical symptoms which medicine has no explanation for or has not been able to cure. You may realise your self-worth, feel empowered through the process of understanding yourself and others as well as the circumstances you have endured in your life, or you may even embrace talents and traits which you have mastered in previous incarnations.

Residue from past life memories can create issues in our lives. You may have a fear of drowning because you drowned in a previous lifetime. You may experience claustrophobia or anxiety because you suffocated in an earlier life. You may carry weight because you were starved or were mistreated in a past life. Perhaps you feel unable to speak in front of others now, because you have been ridiculed or persecuted for stating your beliefs. You may feel unnoticed, disempowered or victimised, and all these feelings and many other issues can originate from incidents that occurred in previous incarnations.

Another important aspect of regression is to understand why we chose our circumstances. Whether that is to drown, or to lose a child early, or why we have a self-centred, distant parent. Regression is a pathway to access your life plan. You will discover why you behave in a certain way and why you may possess challenging traits. You can be sure that events in your life will create opportunities to learn the particular lessons your soul chose this incarnation for.

It is far more effective in eliminating a symptom when a person remembers their situation, rather than being told about it by someone else. Catharsis, or reviewing the memory at the core event, is where miraculous healing is accessed.

You are taking responsibility for yourself and your life by seeking regression, as it opens up a pathway to answer who you really are and why you are here. Whether you experience a past life memory, visit between lives or have a spiritual experience, you can be sure you are in fact communicating with your soul, the eternal, pure part of you that knows everything about your past, present and future.

Toni Reilly is an internationally recognised Past Life facilitator and professional trainer. After training with Dr. Brian Weiss she devised her own unique techniques. As the founder of Toni Reilly Institute she developed the Diploma of SoulLife™ Psychology, a professional qualification for intuitive holistic practitioners. www.tonireillyinstitute.com | www.tonireilly.com.au | info@tonireilly.com.au | + 61 0413 088 970

Healing

For author Serene Conneeley, a trip to South America reveals all kinds of hidden treasures.

I believe the earth is sacred and nature is healing, and I've learned a little about myself, and gained some kind of healing, from every place I've travelled to. From plant medicine ceremonies in the jungles of the Amazon and pagan rituals in the English countryside to meditations inside Egypt's Great Pyramid and spiritual pilgrimages along the leylines of Spain, I've long appreciated the magic of the earth itself to heal us.

The South American country of Brazil is no different. It's a place of powerful crystals, ancient magic, exotic spirituality, lush rainforests, dramatic waterfalls, potent energy and intense vibrations. My journey began in the hot, dry north, a place of sun-soaked, primal energy. Salvador is the centre of Afro-Brasilian culture and of Candomble, a spiritual tradition developed from the rituals introduced by African slaves, the Catholicism they hid their practices within, and the animistic beliefs of the Amerindian people native to this land. I was so grateful to be able to attend a Candomble ritual in the home of a priestess, which was fascinating, with its primitive drum beats, trance dancing and channeling of messages from their deities.

I felt more at home in the south though, at Iguazu Falls, the sacred meeting point of air, land and water (and three separate countries - Brazil, Argentina and Paraguay), and a place of rainbows and wild nature. The thermal resort of Caxambu was also deeply healing, and I felt refreshed and renewed as I soaked in the heated mineral waters of one spring and drank from a cooler source. The twelve different springs all have a different mineral composition (and a different taste!), and are recommended for the treatment of various different ailments - from kidney stones to eye problems, high blood pressure and infertility.

Spiritual travellers also flock to the village of Sao Thome das Letras, which is located on a bed of quartz rock in the mountains and is famous for the number of UFO sightings that have taken place there, as well as for the entrance to a tunnel claimed to burrow all the way to Machu Picchu in Peru, which is kind of spooky to climb down into. Some claim it is one of the seven energy points of the planet, and the vibration of the area is palpable.

But my most profound healing experience took place in the centre of Brazil, the heart of the country, where the energy is nurturing and gentle. Joao Teixeira de Faria, known as John of God, has been healing people for decades in the tiny village of Abadiania. He was guided to build his healing centre, the Casa de Dom Inacio (the House of Saint Ignatius) here because it's located on one of the largest quartz crystal deposits in the world, and quartz amplifies healing vibrations. You can certainly feel the energy of the land here. The gardens surrounding the buildings are a place of immense peace and power, and it's wonderful to just relax under the trees, meditating on the wooden benches, talking to other pilgrims and soaking up the sunshine and the leylines of the earth.

Nearby is a sacred waterfall, and a visit is often prescribed as part of people's treatment. An underground stream flows through the crystal beds beneath the Casa and is purified and charged with energy before splashing down into the waterfall. It's wonderful to submerge yourself in its refreshingly cold and healing waters, gazing up at the sky through the green canopy overhead, absorbing the ancient power of nature, and of the crystals and the earth itself. Some people have visions there; others feel physically, emotionally or spiritually cleansed, and it's considered a sacred place for direct communication with Spirit.

The incredible healing energy of the land in this area is an important part of Joao's work, but so are the visible operations, psychic surgeries and energy work he performs at the Casa. He has cut tumours out of bodies, got wheelchair-bound people walking, cured cancer, blindness and HIV, and facilitated spiritual and emotional healing from grief, depression and psychological disorders. Yet the seventy-three-year-old dubbed the Miracle Man can't read or write and has no medical training. Instead he is a medium, channelling thirty-three different entities, many of them deceased Brazilian doctors and surgeons, as well as the founder of the Jesuits the Casa is named after. It is they who diagnose the thousands of people who flock to Abadiania every week, prescribe the herbal medicines and perform the surgeries. Joao doesn't even remember what he's done at the end of a session - he's an "unconscious medium", giving his body over while he channels the medical experts through. Staff at the Casa can tell which being he is incorporating by his mannerisms, voice and even eye colour, which changes depending on which entity is working through him on a particular day.

I don't know how or why it seems to work; certainly it defies logical explanation and understanding. Joao has been studied by doctors and scientists from around the world, but no one has been able to explain what he does or prove him a fake. He has his sceptics, but it's hard to doubt when you've experienced it yourself and seen it with your own eyes. I witnessed some visible surgeries - which I struggled with because I am squeamish and their gruesome vividness was confronting - and was astounded by the quick recovery and effectiveness for those who had them.

Sometimes our intuition, our bodies, or our dreams tell us when we're on the right (or wrong) path.

I took my mum in the hope Joao could cure her diabetes, so I was surprised, when I went before the entity on my first day, to be told I'd be having an operation that afternoon. Terrified by the prospect of an eye scraping or scissors up the nose, his most common treatment, the whole time I waited to go in I prayed for it to be an invisible surgery. Thankfully, it was. I filed in to a small room with several others and sat in meditation, then Joao came in and said a prayer in Portuguese, asking the entities to heal us. I felt a sensation below my chest - not pain exactly, but discomfort, as though something was being done there. When I went back to my room, where I was instructed to rest for 24 hours, the area was swollen and sore. If I was imagining it, it would not have been there that I pictured something being done. I also felt dazed and vague, much like the after-effects of anaesthesia. In scientific tests of Joao's patients, x-rays have discovered incisions and internal stitches in people who've had invisible operations.

After resting, I spent the next day and a half in current - when visitors are not having an operation, they sit in the surrounding room, meditating in order to raise the vibration and send energy to Joao and the entities. I went back for revision the following week and sat in the current room again, spent time at the sacred waterfall, had a crystal bed session, and went before Joao with a photo of a sick friend, who was prescribed herbal medicine. I was also prescribed herbs for 55 days, along with slight dietary changes.

My migraines did improve for a while, although I was not cured. Nor, unfortunately, was my mum. But we met people who had been diagnosed with terminal illnesses and dramatically cured by Joao, including a woman who was riddled with cancer and told she would soon die - she's since dedicated her life to helping him as a volunteer - an American man crippled with arthritis, who was slowly beginning to walk again, the woman who ran our pousada, who was cured of a brain tumour, and an Aussie healed of a near-fatal heart murmur. We also met an amazing Brazilian woman who'd travelled to the Casa in search of both emotional and physical healing. When she saw Joao he told her to start painting for him. She replied that she had no artistic talent, but he insisted she did now - and she could suddenly paint the most beautiful healing artworks, which gave her an income as well as a purpose.

Meeting fellow pilgrims is definitely a huge part of the experience, and a wonderful sense of camaraderie develops with the other people who are there hoping to be healed. Visitors swap stories, share experiences, and lend support as each person goes through their individual process. The healings here are not always what you would expect. Some are far more subtle, or address a different issue, but just being in the energy of this place, in this land, with these people, is an experience I will always treasure.

Serene Conneeley is a Sydney writer and healer. She's the author of Seven Sacred Sites: Magical Journeys That Will Change Your Life, Witchy Magic, Mermaid Magic and the Into the Mists Trilogy, is a reconnective healing practitioner, and has studied magical and medicinal herbalism, bereavement counselling and reiki, as well as politics and journalism.
Website: www.SereneConneeley.com.

Faery Reiki

Nicola McIntosh

I have only recently discovered Faery Reiki. I stumbled across it purely by accident, but in saying that, there really are no accidents are there?

How does Faery Reiki differ from other Reiki?

In my personal opinion, energy is energy, so really there is no big difference. All Reikis follow the same principles and are conducted mainly the same way whereby the practitioner uses certain symbols to activate certain energy/healing. The healing flows through the practitioner as they are the conduit. It should not come from their own energy field. Faery Reiki has its specific set of Reiki symbols as well that are symbolic of different Faery energies. The only difference with Faery Reiki is the way in which the practitioner works with the chakras. Normally in Reiki you do each chakra in order, but with Faery Reiki there is a specific sequence. Violet Paille is the founder of Faery Reiki and was shown the method by the faery that gave her the symbols. She believes the method is pure and unadulterated and therefore asks that it is not changed.

I received my attunement from overseas. I was sent the attunement in a Chi bubble that I had to tune into when I was able to spare half an hour to meditate and receive it. I wasn't sure what to expect at all. I lay down and asked for the Faery attunement to take place. First I saw an Apple tree and then I was lying under the Apple Tree. As I lay there I sensed gold dust being sprinkled all over me and out of the dust I could see a stunning Faery in front of me. She was wearing all white and had white hair. She had large, black eyes and very dark brown skin. She blew me a kiss and said 'Welcome'. I then felt compelled to use Reiki on myself at the time and when I came out of the meditation I felt so alive! I was seriously buzzing for days afterwards. I had this amazing abundance of energy which I used to cleanse the house and went on bush walks and generally just revelled in the feeling. I found out later that the Apple tree is representative of Avalon, the Faery Isle, which was great confirmation for me that I was not making it up.

Can anyone use Faery Reiki?

I do wonder about this one. I'm not one to normally put limits on such things, but I have found that with anything Faery, you must be pure of heart with good intent. This is the only time they will really work with you in my experience. However in saying that, I am no authority on the subject.

Even if you haven't had an attunement with Faery Reiki, you can still work with Faery energy. All you need do is ask and start to attune yourself to Nature. They do like to help. We can call on this energy wherever we live, for as we know, there are no boundaries with energy. It does help us if we are out in Nature to be able to perceive it easier, but we can still experience it if we live in a city or apartment.

How can we work with Faery energy?

You can start by honouring and welcoming Faery into your house or garden. If you live in the city, you could put some plants on your balcony with a few little Faery crystals or ornaments of mushrooms or Faery doors etc. You might like to put up some lead crystals that bring rainbows into your home or things that are sparkly. Or you could bring nature to you by collecting stones or branches from places you travel to and arrange them in an area like an altar or a special place set aside for them. I like to create wands from branches I find out in Nature and I use them to connect back to the place where I found them by meditating with them in my hand. It can be an amazing experience when you connect to the tree the branch actually came from.

One of the most important things when walking in nature is to walk quietly. I go bushwalking every week by myself. I'm amazed at how people can do an entire walk talking to someone all the way. To tune in, you need to listen. You need to be quiet and receptive. Listen to the wind in the trees, listen to all the birds. You'll find after a while you become a part of the landscape, and insects and animals will end up being so close to you that they are not fazed in the slightest with your presence. Also, when I enter the forest, I picture my aura expanding and disappearing into the trees, and I announce myself when I enter and ask to please connect to the area. I ask my guides and the Fae to be with me while I walk, and find that I receive so much guidance and information whilst walking that it becomes a very magical experience. Even if you live in a city, you can always find a park or a single tree to connect to. Sit under a tree when you have lunch and talk to it. I communicate in my mind without physically verbalising it. Trees can take a while to communicate back, if ever, but persevere. Sometimes you just need to show it you are dedicated to communicating to it.

The more and more you connect to Nature, the more you will be able to perceive Faery energy. They are closely tied into the Landscape, so this is the first step

Artwork credit - Nicola McIntosh ©2013

CRYSTAL Q&A

Crystals for Connecting with Nature

Tuning into Nature starts with your Heart Chakra. Not only is it how you connect with the world around you, but it is associated with the colour Green, just like the predominant colour of Forests & Plants. Here is a sample of what you might like to work with:

Emerald - Emerald is a favourite of the Faeries. A perfect stone to attune to Nature through your Heart Chakra because it is also known as the 'stone of successful love'. It enhances unity, which is exactly what we are after when attuning to Nature Spirits. When you come with a pure and open heart, they will see this.

Moss Agate - Moss Agate has a very strong connection to Nature. It is a very stabilising stone and is a perfect stone for anyone that works outdoors. Being a green stone, it is also a stone of abundance. Meditate with this stone or carry it with you when walking in Nature and ask for it to help you connect to your surroundings.

Rainforest Jasper - Rainforest Jasper is a beautiful stone that connects you to the Earth as well as to Nature. It helps you to anchor yourself once again, and works with Base, Spleen and Heart Chakras. A great stone for healers to use to help re-activate herbal healing knowledge from plants.

If you have a crystal question you would like answered in our next issue, please email Nicola directly at: nicola@spiritstone.com.au. (Please keep in mind that not every question may be able to be answered in each edition).

in finding your way to them. They will show themselves to you when you are really ready.

There are also Faery meditations you can do that will help with your connections. One of my favourites is Brian and Wendy Froud's Pathway to Faery app.

There are also many books on Faery, and if you truly want to learn about what real Faery energy is, you can research The Sidhe (pronounced Shee). This is the original Faery race from Celtic tradition. Unfortunately the Victorian era romanticised what Faery looked like and this has now become so common place that it is hard to convince a sceptic to believe that the original Faery race still exists and that they are very large in stature, but have pulled themselves away from Humans because we have become more and more separate from Nature. As with any Nature spirit or Fae being, they will show themselves to us in a form that is recognisable for us to comprehend, therefore they show themselves Human like. This form is less threatening for us. They are energetic beings - if they showed themselves to us as they truly are, we would not be able to comprehend what we were seeing.

I must say though, one thing I have noticed is that when you attune to a specific energy, you tend you have this 'Wow' moment, but when you try again, it's never as pronounced as when you first attuned to it. This can give you the feeling that maybe you have lost the connection. I've come to learn that once you have made the connection, you never lose it. But it helps to keep working with the energy to strengthen the connection and make yourself more familiar with it.

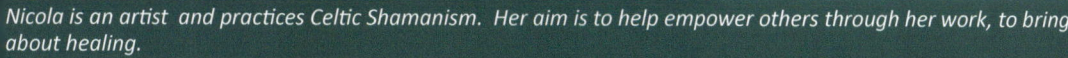

Nicola is an artist and practices Celtic Shamanism. Her aim is to help empower others through her work, to bring about healing.

Contact Nicola at: www.spiritstone.com.au / www.nicolamcintosh.com

Karina Machado is the author of three books - Spirit Sisters, Where Spirits Dwell and her latest Love Never Dies, where she explores the transformative effects of After-Death contact.

Alex Cayas seeks to understand how for all of us, love transcends death with speaking to Australian author Karina Machado.

Through her research for her three books and over 200 interviews conducted, Karina is now speaking to audiences about these effects - sharing stories, experiences and patterns she has noticed with her talk *"The Power of Love: The Transformative Effects of After-Death Contact."*

Karina will be appearing and presenting this talk at the upcoming Afterlife Explores Conference in January and at Paracon Australia 2015 in May.

I had the pleasure of discussing some of these ideas with Karina further.

Alex: When I think After-Death contact, my first thought is mediums. Can you take us through your definition and experiences outside mediumship featured in Love Never Dies and in your presentation?

Karina: While mediums can facilitate after-death contact, and many of my subjects have received solace from readings with mediums, my presentation will focus primarily on spontaneous moments of after-death contact, which can encompass a wide range of phenomena. These include smelling a loved one's perfume, hearing their voice, having a powerful dream, moments of synchronicity such as hearing their favourite song and via symbolic motifs, like seeing a butterfly in the depths of winter, feeling their touch and seeing an apparition of the deceased.

A: Where did your interest begin in exploring After-Death contact? Was it a personal experience of your own?

K: No, for me what made me delve into this, and what eventually put me on the road to writing Love Never Dies, was my growing interest in this particular kind of story. My interest started in childhood. As a child, mum shared with me some experiences of precognition where she was forewarned about the deaths of two of her loved ones, and I guess this planted the seed of interest in me about the bonds of love and how they could stretch perception. All of my work leading up to Love Never Dies touches on the theme.

A: You've entered many people's personal stories and heard them describe their journey to you. Can you share the healing effects After-Death contact has had on those you've connected with?

K: As my interviewees have explained to me, the healing effects can range from an immediate "lifting of mood" on a bad day, to the very powerful effect of preventing

LOVE NEVER DIES
– an interview with Karina Machado

them from taking their own life. One lady told me how one day, months after her son had died in a car accident, she was weeping in her kitchen, having what she called one of her bad days. Suddenly, she saw his smiling face materialise in front of her, and while it gave her a bit of a shock, she immediately felt a million times better, the sadness momentarily lifted. In another story, a woman who'd shared a very powerful bond with her grandmother felt her presence at her side when she was in hospital, following the miscarriage of her baby. Knowing that her grandmother was with her not only showed her that her nan's love for her was as strong as ever, that she still cared, but helped her deal with the grief of losing her baby.

A: Are these transformative effects only noticed and experienced by those grieving a recent loss or does it have a wider reach?

K: The transformative effects have a wider reach. Primarily, they transform the bereaved person who has the after-death contact, offering healing and hope, and giving them the impetus to go on in the wake of deepest loss. In this case, they are a much-needed light in the dark. In a more far-reaching way, hearing (as in my case) or reading about experiences of after-death contact with a loved one provide a sense of hope and perspective, and may usher in an awakening spirituality -a journey which for me is ongoing.

A: Your work (both books and talks) has a strong focus on the theme of love. Can you talk more about love as a force that lives on after death?

K: The stories in my book suggest that love doesn't end with the death of the body. In fact, some of the accounts indicate that it only grows! One chapter looks at the enduring bonds of family; for instance, a woman who died at a young age returns to help her daughter settle her babies when new motherhood threatened to overwhelm her. In other stories, after-death contact works as a healing salve on a troubled relationship, improving and strengthening a fractured bond, and healing old wounds in the bereaved person left behind. Sometimes, the effects are far less subtle, with loved ones acting as "guardian angels" and stepping in to prevent danger or death. In one case, a woman repeatedly dreamt of her late father urging her to go to the doctor, as he stroked his throat. The dreams became so persistent that she finally heeded his warning and discovered that she had the beginnings of thyroid cancer.

A: You mentioned that researching and hearing these stories has had a transformative effect on you. How has this transformation manifested through your work as a writer?

K: When I was researching my first book, Spirit Sisters, I had a life-changing moment when I interviewed a lady called Kath, who'd lost her two young daughters in an horrific car accident. I remember finishing the interview and thinking, 'I will never be the same again.' Her story of seeing her lovely girls drift towards her like snowflakes in the dark room, on the night that she'd resolved to end her life, immediately changed me. (Of course it transformed Kath first, she didn't go through with her plan and has gone on to have another child). I went straight to hug my children and thought 'I'll show love wherever possible." I remember feeling so honoured by the gift she'd given me. I hope that by sharing these stories in my book, my readers will be similarly moved and transformed.

In a broader sense, I am now inspired to make the most of the life I've been given. In stories of after-death contact there are powerful lessons for the living. For me, these lessons involve being more loving, compassionate and kind towards all people, not just my loved ones.

A: You're now speaking to audiences about the ideas covered in your latest book Love Never Dies with the presentation "The Power of Love: The Transformative Effects of After-Death Contact". Could we have a sneak peak as to what the presentation will look like?

K: This presentation will draw on what I've learned throughout the seven or so years that I've been writing about everyday people's experiences of the paranormal. Through the process of doing close to 200 interviews across three books, I learned that certain experiences were not scary or confronting, but rather, comforting and healing. These experiences invariably involved people seeing, sensing or feeling the spirit of a late loved one. Eventually, I became so intrigued by how profound and powerful these experiences were that I decided to dedicate a whole book to them, Love Never Dies, which was released in July. As well as celebrating the significance of these beautiful experiences, and how they changed my subjects' lives for the better - in some cases, reversing their decision to escape their grief by taking their own life - the book documents how I too was transformed by these stories. My subjects' experiences became the catalyst for my own search for a more spiritual and meaningful way of life.

A: The carousel keeps turning. What is the next adventure?

K: There are ideas brewing, that's for sure! My research work has added to my burgeoning desire to explore my heritage. I was born in Uruguay and I surprised myself by the extent to which a yearning for the country of my birth (and the loved ones left behind, like living ghosts) worked itself into my latest book and I'd like to explore this further, either in memoir or fiction. Speaking of fiction, I'd like to try my hand at something that draws on my many years of interviewing people who've had firsthand encounters of the most extraordinary kind. However, there's nothing in the works just yet. Yet - watch this space!

Alex Cayas is a writer, host/producer of Ghosts of Oz podcast and director of Paracon Australia. Alex also founded and runs Missing Piece Productions and Management.

Artwork Credit – Nicolle Poll

Lunar New Year - The Year of the Wood Sheep

Steadily stepping into the Year of the Wood Sheep, Nicolle Poll gives an insight of the energies it brings on what promises to be a stabilising and progressive year ahead.

Welcome to the 2015 Lunar Year of the Wood Sheep, also known as the Year of the Green Sheep, Goat or Ram. Based on the Chinese Lunar Calendar, Chinese New Year commences on the new moon of 19th February 2015 and ends on 7th February 2016, though it falls on a different day each year on the international Gregorian Calendar. It is known as Lunar New Year outside of China.

The Sheep is the eighth sign of the Chinese Zodiac, which consists of twelve animal signs. Each sign is featured for a year, creating a twelve year cycle for the zodiac to progress through all the signs. Within each animal sign, there is a cycle of the five elements - metal, water, wood, fire and earth. Within this cycle, it takes sixty years (5 elements x 12 year cycle) before the same animal sign and element is experienced again, with the last Wood Sheep cycle being in 1955.

The luck day for Wood Sheep year is Tuesday, the Fixed Element is Fire, the colour is Green, Summer is the power season and being the eighth sign in the Chinese Zodiac is a good aspect as '8' is considered a lucky number and brings prosperity and peace. The Sheep Years for the past century are 1919, 1931, 1943, 1955, 1967, 1979, 1991, 2003 and 2015.

For Sheep people, it is your year, so expect a fortuitous, successful year ahead! It is a time for progress and connecting with others, both professionally and personally. Travel and vacations are favourable. Sheep people are strong and stable, good decision makers and adaptable, they enjoy being in the company of groups and are honest and emphatic to the needs of others.

On a personal level for everyone, the positive aspect of this Wood Sheep Year brings with it business success for careers and ventures, and is positive for serious relationships, family, fertility, mental and physical health, creativity, travel and finances, though be mindful of overspending. A crucial year as it brings stability to political situations, economic growth and, with hard work and diligence, brings about prosperity.

On a national and global level the steadiness of a Wood Sheep Year has powerful influences that will reverberate back to us all on a personal level. It brings with it economic growth coupled with stability, with education and environmental issues gaining focus. There will be attention on inter-country relations on a world scale, with the shifting of war tensions and underlying political systems.

It will be an innovative year for technology as huge advancements will be made that will affect society as we know it, and we will live with these influences for years to come. Current technologies will become more available to everyone. Space exploration will alter our existing knowledge of the Universe as we know it, and current information will also need to be rewritten.

2015 is about being prepared, and is the year of small, though consistent changes. Life under the Wood Sheep takes on a positive flow after the more trying energies of the previous Wood Horse and Water Snake years, and it is an important time to not only enjoy the relief that this peace and harmony brings, but to put in place measures to protect you through the down times that come with life. Sheep cannot move sideways or backwards, only forward - energetically the Wood Sheep Year takes on this characteristic, allowing you to keep moving forward in your life.

It is a time to value and nurture quality connections with family and friends, and time to nurture yourself. Sheep energy is empowering to connect with as they are hardy and natural survivors, will adapt and live in the harshest conditions and climates and not only survive, they thrive. Use this power to move yourself and your own life forward in the ways you want to most.

The shadow aspect of the Wood Sheep Year brings the caution of overspending from enjoying too much the stable economic energies, and not maximizing the steady energies it brings with it. Calculated and considered risks with investments are recommended. Fertility is enhanced in a Wood Sheep year, making it a positive time for conception and bringing new life into the world, though be mindful of contraception if not planning on family additions.

The stability of the Wood Sheep Year is a great opportunity to get your world sorted! Make space for personal time - whether to replenish your own energies or enjoy and explore creative yearnings. Take a good look at your life and organise your own personal domain where it is needed most - whether it be with family, friends and loved ones, family planning, making decisions about your education, work or business direction, sorting out personal finances, clarifying and making goals to ensure you are the creator and manager of your life and life is not managing you, clearing clutter from your daily environments and freshening up your home, connecting with your own creativity and spending time in the natural world around you.

Nicolle Poll is a regular contributor and part of the inSpirit creative team. Nicolle works as an Artist specialising in Oracle Cards, Totemic Animal illustrations and Soul Journey portraits, also having studied and practised a wide range of modalities in her personal and spiritual development.

Contact Nicolle at: Email: artworkbynicolle@bigpond.com or **Facebook:** www.facebook.com/ArtworkByNicolle

Cosmic Codes
with Amanda Coppa

Moon Magic for the months ahead.

The moon represents our emotions, feelings, femininity, intuition and unconscious. Every month the moon waxes and wanes in regular cycles. Paying attention to the moon cycles allows us to work with its energy rather than against it. During every month we have both a new moon (new beginnings) and full moon (release & closure) which supports us in establishing new patterns whilst clearing outdated ones from our life.

JANUARY 2015

2:54pm AEST Monday 5

Under the Cancer full moon our feelings, instincts and emotional responses are heightened. Our sensitivity to energy is increased, and we are drawn to connecting more intimately with others. Our thoughts turn to our family and personal relationships, how we are really feeling and what meaning that brings to us. Old issues can resurface now and we need to express our deeper feelings rather than bottling them up. It's important to honour your feelings and flow with the energy around you.

Tip for Cancerians: Learn from your experiences and open up to your true potential.

11:14pm AEST Wednesday 21

New Moons are an ideal time for setting intentions and focusing on new beginnings. The new moon in the progressive sign of Aquarius is ideal for networking, connecting with the community/social groups, and making new friends. If you've been wanting to try something a little different, now is the time to break away from old patterns and commit to the new and true. Even if it's a little unconventional, trust your ideas and follow through with your inspiration.

Tip for Aquarians: Self-awareness and self-control is the key to your success so back yourself and do it your way!

FEBRUARY 2015

9:09am AEST Wednesday 4

With the full moon in the creative and fun-loving sign of Leo, this is the perfect time to open up our desire to create, experiment and explore. Recognising your talents, abilities and potential is strong at this time. Just be sure to recognise this in others too! Under the full moon you may be tempted to rush in where angels fear to tread. Remember that tact, consideration and teamwork will make all the difference.

Tip for Leos: Do your best to avoid tension and drama at this time, instead let love be your guide.

9:47am AEST Thursday 19

With a second new moon in Aquarius this year we are given the green light to steady ourselves, clarify our goals and step forward with confidence. It's important for us to tune in and trust our inner knowing in order to bring new ideas into being. Assisting others and working collectively as a team will grant additional support and benefits. Strong decisions need to be made, and perhaps a fresh approach to tackling old issues.

Tip for Aquarians: Pay attention to all the good things that are occurring around you right now.

MARCH 2015

4:06am AEST Friday 6

The full moon in the analytical and self-aware sign of Virgo highlights our ability to think rationally and assess situations from a practical perspective. It brings new insights and solutions to old problems, which will help us get on top of things and move forward with greater ease. Staying focused and being patient while you address any lingering issues will help. This is a great time to seek out areas where there is lack or excess and concentrate on bringing them into balance.

Tip for Virgos: Habits are difficult to change but with courage and inner strength you can do it.

7:36pm AEST Friday 20

With the new moon in the intuitive and compassionate sign of Pisces it's a wonderful opportunity to connect with your deeper side and honour your inner feelings. Intuition and emotional wellbeing are heightened and it's well worth taking time out for quiet inner reflection and tuning in to the messages from Spirit. Things may not be what they first seem right now so take your time and feel your way. This new moon also coincides with a solar eclipse bringing about change and adjustment on a deep personal level.

Tip for Pisces: Your hopes and dreams give direction and enthusiasm to your life.

Amanda Coppa is a heart-centred crystal healer who incorporates astrology, numerology, Reiki and oracle cards into her work. She is passionate about self-healing, empowerment and helping you understand the REAL you.

Connect with Amanda at http://www.facebook.com/cosmiccodes.

Divine Healing through Dreaming

There are many ways to heal your mind, body and spirit. Most people seek their healing through the aid of someone else; an energy healer, a doctor, or a professional new age guru! You may pay these professionals for energetic healing, nutritional advice, past life regressions, and spiritual counselling, and YES you can find much healing with the help of these people. BUT there is also another way - YOU are your own healer! There is already so much healing wisdom within you and this wisdom is trying to get through to you every night through DREAMING! Dreaming is magic in its purest form; unaffected by the conscious mind and ego, the messages we receive in our dreams are straight to the point, to the core of a problem that may be present in our lives. It may be your health physically, it may be a toxic relationship or workplace you are in, it may be a part of your true self you are denying - your sub-conscious mind is seeking balance, wholeness, love and happiness without a price tag!

In our dreams we can journey through realms of endless possibilities, fulfil wishes, travel through time and space visiting past lives even future ones, AND we can bring inspiration, healing, clarity and knowledge of ourselves and our life's purpose back into our waking lives! Each dream dreamt up by you has sacred symbols to decipher and once you learn the dreaming language, you have yourself a powerful ally in healing and magic.

I have been recording my dreams for over 20 years. From a young age my dreams captured and romanced me. I found myself enchanted by the dream realm, swept up in my love for its mysterious ways, and I would eagerly prepare for sleep, excited by what my own mind would bring back to the waking world. I quickly discovered patterns within the dream scenes, symbols and keys to unlocking my subconscious mind.

Within my dreaming realm I met with and communed with my ancestors, I revisited past lives and discovered new and fantastical lands, I would hang out with Gods and Goddesses, and I was blessed with divine spiritual healings. I even saw frightening demons and found the courage deep within to face my fears coming through as nightmares! Dreams were the doorway into my core and my own healing MAGIC!

Most people say they don't remember any dreams or simply don't dream at all but that is not true! In fact everyone dreams up to 7 dreams per night! When you focus upon your dreams, connect and become aware of this, the more dreams you will be able to remember, the more vivid your dreams will become. We have unlimited potential in our dreams. We can do and go to whatever and wherever we would like! WHY, oh why anyone would ever wake up and simply forget this magical world is way beyond me!

Not only amazing and magical, dreams actually are very important to keeping our minds healthy and functioning well. The first dreams we have at night are usually our brains sorting though what has happened in our lives each day, filing away memories and things we have learnt that day to access at some other time if needed. Once these sorting dreams have passed we go into a deep sleep where dreams are surreal and may contain awesome wish fulfilment or fear facing nightmares (there is light and dark sides to all magic, dreams included!)

Most of the dreams we remember happen in the morning just before waking up. I have found that you can almost catch a dream by the tail to remember it! If you can just see a slither, pull a thread, feel a feeling, you can hold a puzzle piece in your mind and then the dream will all come flooding back.

Your sub-consciousness speaks to you though symbols. You must become a dream detective and figure out the clues. The dream symbols can be taken quite literally. For instance, if you dream of a dog, think about what a dog means to you, your connection to dogs, your memories of dogs; is it a positive or a negative dream symbol? Only you know the answer. If you have a good relationship to dogs then this dream symbol may mean companionship, loyalty, caring. If you are fearful of dogs then it may mean an enemy or someone may be acting like a "bitch". The dream dog may be showing you aspects of yourself perhaps. If the snarling, biting dog is being kept in a cage, are you keeping your negative emotions caged within?

> *Not only amazing and magical, dreams actually are very important to keeping our minds healthy and functioning well.*

YOUR DREAM JOURNAL

Begin your healing dream journey by writing your dreams down. If you come across a symbol that baffles you, try word association; write it down and then write down feelings, memories, associated words that follow until you get that light bulb moment! That AH HA! The puzzle piece clicks! Any book can become a dream journal - you do not need it to be fancy or beautiful. It could start with simple scraps of paper or perhaps a word document on your computer if that is your style, but I feel the more energy you spend on making your dream journal special and magical, the more you will focus on dreaming and in a way you will be programming your brain to remember. Use a fresh sprig of Rosemary as a page marker as this fragrant, radiant herb will sharpen your ability to remember your dreams. Another item to help with your dream journaling is a special pen dedicated to dream jotting. Keep these items on your dream altar.

YOUR MAGICAL DREAM ALTAR

Setting up a dream altar within your bedroom is a great way to connect to the dream realms. Upon a small table, shelf or even a blanket box, place a cloth of colours such as a lavender, purple, dreamy blue, or perhaps even black for the night sky. You could scatter it with silver glitter stars if you like. Place dream time herbs - Rosemary for remembering and Lavender for calming relaxation, sage and jasmine buds for prophetic dreaming. They can be fresh or dried herbs. You may also add, if you like, some small Willow tree twigs as this tree connects to dreams, feminine energy and Lunar magic, Healing and dreaming Crystals such as Amethyst to connect to your subconscious and psychic sensors - clear quartz for clarity, Apophyllite for astral travelling, black obsidian and black tourmaline can be added to absorb any night time negativity. Humanly, naturally collected Animal medicines such as Feathers, Fur, shells and Bones can be placed upon your altar if you like - Owl medicine to connect to night magic and wisdom, black Crow for connecting to your ancestors and receiving messages from the other side, perhaps some Hare fur for connecting to the moon. This is YOUR magical dream Altar - begin to place things of sentimental value to YOU upon this sacred space. Animal totems and spirit guides can be represented, Gods and Goddesses such as Hypnos, Greek God of sleep and dreams, or the Ancient Egyptian Goddess of the night sky, Nuit, or any God or Goddess you are connected to. Adorn your altar with items symbolising the dreamscape, representing dream magic and healing. To use your dream altar each night change the sacred items according to your intentions, light a white, black or silver candle to focus and affirm your intentions to remember your dreams (don't forget to blow it out before sleeping!). If you had a question you wanted answered you could write it down in your dream journal and place it on your altar and in the morning write down the guidance you received through the night. Each morning write out your dream and spend time in front of your dream altar reflecting and piecing your dream clues together and thank any guides who are helping you to heal and become whole through dreaming.

With the aid of your dreams you are now your own healer of mind, body and spirit.

Wishing you all a Blessed sleep and sweet dreams ~ love Natashaxx

Natasha Heard is a creatress of all things magical! A natural witch ~ her magical life and connection to the Earth flow into all her creations. Specialising in Wands, Sceptres and Staves; and creating with her horticulturalist husband Michael, Blessed Rune sets and Tree of Life Bind Rune Talismans. Her innate connection with all aspects of the natural world and passion for magic is what makes her a true creatress of powerful, magical tools.

Natasha can be contacted Email: blessedbranches@gmail.com or Facebook: Blessed Branches...magical tools by Natasha Heard.

The Healer

Going within reveals all the answers, as this short story by Jude Downes demonstrates.

One inspired spring day, the healer felt pulled to visit the local well. As she filled her bucket with the cool clear water, she was approached by a man in a long white robe. He spoke to her softly, and yet his rich deep voice reverberated in every part of her. He said 'I was sent to help you.'

The healer stared at him for a few moments before asking 'In what way can you help me?'

'I was sent to offer you the gift of enlightenment, but first, you must complete three tasks'.

The healer had never experienced anybody like this man and yet he seemed familiar. With his piercing blue eyes he appeared ageless. They seemed to bore straight into her soul - as though he knew everything there was to know about her.

Instead of fear she felt as though she were in the presence of an old friend. His manner was all-encompassing as well as warm and loving. Although the healer had just met him, she had total trust in what he was about to ask of her.

The man said 'When you return to your home, you are to go within for seven days and seven nights and think of nothing. This is your first task.'

'When you have accomplished this, your second task is to go into nature and listen to the birds, to the trees and to the wind and the streams.'

'When you have completed both of these tasks successfully, I will return to inform you of your third and last task.'

The healer could only nod in affirmation as she inhaled deeply before finally turning to head for home.

She began to prepare herself for her first task. She went into her sanctuary; her healing space, to light a candle and create an ambient setting for this task.

'This shouldn't be too hard' she thought. 'I'm a healer. I am aware of the spiritual nature of all things.'

As the healer lay down on her own healing table and prepared to go within, she suddenly remembered people she had promised to see. The healer thought to herself 'Well, it doesn't have to begin right now; I will begin after I've seen my friends.'

When she returned, she lay down in her special place and closed her eyes. There was a knock at the door.

She went to answer it and again rejected the need to go within. Each time she attempted to go within and think no thoughts, something would announce its arrival in her head or her environment and deter her from the task the man at the well had set for her.

'I can't do this' she thought. 'I believed I was spiritual enough to do anything that was asked of me. I can't even pass the first task.'

Having recognised the problem of putting everything else first instead of the needs of the self, the healer was well on the way to completing her first task.

Next she ventured into nature thinking what an easy task this would be. She had been into nature many times and heard the sounds of the birds, the rustling leaves of the trees as they swayed in the breeze, the trickling of the streams as they meandered over smooth rocks and the whistling of the wind on a stormy day. Task number two was a cinch!

As the healer wandered deeper into the bush, she became aware of a silence she had never before experienced. As she listened to the silence, she slowly awakened her senses to other sounds.

Instead of the normal sounds a bird makes, or a tree or stream or the wind, she heard words and songs. There were messages coming from all around her.

'So this is what the man in the white robe wanted me to experience.' It was beyond her imagination; beyond her limited view of the spiritual nature of all life. 'What a wonderful task he had set for me.'

The healer returned to the well where she again met the white-robed man. He was already aware of how she had fared on her first two tasks. The answer to both shone from her heart, her eyes and her whole being.

Jude Downes, author of 'From Grief to Goddess' book and Healing Cards, is passionate about helping others access their inner realms to write new chapters in their life story. Jude's intimate connection to Mother Earth and the messages that come from nature weave a path in the unity between mind, body, soul and emotions to form the foundations of her business 'Dreaming the Seed' and her formula for successful goal creation.
Jude is a Psycho Spiritual Hypnotherapist, a Colour Therapist and Clairvoyant.
Contact Jude at: Web: www.fromgrieftogoddess.com

For the love of Angels

By Suzanne Hartas

Her face glowed with the sheer joy of experience.

'Task number three' he told her 'is to take the knowledge you have learned from your first two tasks and apply them to your healing work.'

He announced that he would return in one years' time.

With renewed confidence, the healer began incorporating her newfound knowledge into healing. However not everyone wanted to know about these things.

She became disheartened. How was she going to complete task number three when people wouldn't accept what she was trying to do?

Suddenly a thought occurred to her. Why not go within to find the answer; why not visit nature and ask the birds, the trees, the streams and the wind?

The healer did these things and was told the following message.

> Heal with your heart
> And let others accept love
> If they want to experience
> The joys your knowledge can bring.
>
> If unable to accept;
> Feel safe and secure
> Knowing you have done all you can
> To bring joy to their hearts and souls.
>
> Renewed with hope, the healer continued to work in this way.

One year later, the healer again went to the well and met the man in the long white robe.

He told her she had travelled far along the path of enlightenment. She had already received the gift of enlightenment by opening herself up to the messages of spirit.

'If we do not seek reward' he said, 'we shall be rewarded when we least expect it. Our soul is always waiting to help us'. The man placed one hand on his heart and the other on the heart of the healer. 'It doesn't matter if it is by a well or within our own heart; our soul guidance is always ready to enlighten us.'

The healer closed her eyes and felt the peace of her experience. When she opened them once more, the man was gone. She knew she would not see him again as she had understood the lessons he had taught her.

Smiling contentedly to herself, the healer felt ready to immerse herself in the joy of living her life fully connected to her soul's guidance. She just needed to remember three things - to go within, to connect fully with nature and to let others experience their own journey through life however they choose to live it.

HEALING LIGHT OF LOVE

Dear blessed children of the light, the dawning of days anew is upon you now. Rest easy in the waters of calm, for the vigorous seas of healing transformation is slowing to a gentle ebb as the flow of healing light blankets you now.

Your soul has lovingly guided you through the challenging currents within the birthing canals toward new life. This necessary rebirth required the letting go of the illusion of the self you once held and freeing the pathways for your God-self to radiate forth.

As you emerge as your Divine self into your vibrant new world of higher consciousness, celebrate your journey into the oneness and allow your light to shine forth as a beacon for others, so they too may feel the stir of desire to know and awaken their God-self within.

Your heaven on Earth is unfolding before your eyes Dear Ones.

Behold the beauty of your world before you and behold the beauty of you, for you are the Divine's most magnificent creation, and in knowing this truth of your perfection, so you shall know peace. For you are the beating heart of God, and it is with much gratitude we thank you for opening your beautiful hearts and joining with us as One Heart, enabling the Divine's healing light of love to flow abundantly through you upon your Earth.

Rest now our Beloved Ones in the comfort of the Father's heart of love as we lovingly assist you in adjusting to the new vibration energies and language of love, peace and harmony.

Many blessings and much love.

Susanne Hartas is a Psychic Medium and Angel Intuitive.

Please contact Suzanne at: www.inspiritmagazine.com; mail@inspiritmagazine.com

Healing Your Soul in a Chaotic World

Amanda Roussety, IPA 2013 Psychic of the Year NSW inSpires us to take a little time and responsibility for our self healing.

Our modern day lives are filled with chaos. Everywhere we turn there is disaster, aggression, tension, and grief in one form or another. People are suffering effects of these globally chaotic and traumatic situations, while on top of that each and every person is trying to deal with their own personal traumas.

We all know someone who is suffering from depression, someone who is grieving, someone who is sick or dying. The list is endless. And what we don't often think about is how seeing a loved one go through these experiences ultimately affects us. We think that if we aren't experiencing it, then we are free of it, but that's where we are wrong. It takes a rare individual to go through life not caring about his fellow man. So often we feel helpless watching those we love sink deeper into a pit of sadness, pain and ultimately emptiness.

So what sort of things lead us to a point of emotional, mental or physical breakdown? The point when we cannot seem to see light in our tunnel of darkness. So many factors can contribute to a final melting point, and in my experience, it is usually a culmination of life experiences that brings this about. Sure we can have something major happen that can start the ball rolling, but many other factors determine the ultimate long term outcome, and this usually comes down to how we see ourselves and the situation presented.

Healing is a multi-layered process, and our inability to get in touch with how we really feel is causing a lot of issues in many people. We are a society afraid to grieve, afraid to feel and afraid to express our emotions for fear of being perceived as weak.

Many traditional cultures spend days and weeks in mourning after the loss of a loved one or a traumatic experience. They openly express their pain, and with total support from all around them. But in modern society we do not allow ourselves to do this. After a loved one passes, we focus on the funeral and then immediately return to work and a 'normal' existence. We hold it together to get the job done, but inside, our soul is crying out in pain. Over time this only causes the energetic layers of our aura to become disrupted and blocked. When the energy doesn't flow it becomes polluted and that pollution leads to imbalances (energetic dis-ease).

If we clear through and rebalance, then energy flows, allowing an optimum chance of full healing and recovery. Healing should be looked at in many areas, and humanity must learn again how to feel, express and see emotion as a normal process, not a foreign one.

What is it to be healed really? Is it to place a Band-Aid over the physical issue and hope for the best, or is it getting to the root of all problems and promoting long term healing so that you can be free of the problem?

We are not just physical bodies; we are a complex system of energetic patterns that affect our thoughts, our emotions and so many other aspects of our physical makeup. We cannot continue to only regard one area of healing as sufficient and assume that the problems will now go away forever. Unless we deal with all areas we are only temporarily delaying a possible return to illness.

Both my partner Mark Coleman and I are healers, and when we created our business 'Infinite Soul' in Narellan, we wanted a space that allowed for healing and spiritual growth on many levels. It was very apparent to us the need for humanity to embrace their deeper self and be awakened to their full potential.

During one of my spiritual healing sessions, I look at not only the current physical problem, but where it originated from or perhaps what is stopping it from healing. It may genuinely be an issue that simply 'happened' to the person. For example they may have been injured and now suffer pain and discomfort. But I need to look at all energetic layers for signs of imbalance and disruption.

Humanity needs to once again become responsible for their own healing journey. They must be willing to face what's really going on inside in order to release and heal properly.

Amanda Roussety is a Celebrity Psychic Medium & Spiritual development Teacher. Accomplishments include becoming a finalist on channel sevens 'The One' and being the NSW Psychic of the Year 2013. Amanda is the cofounder of Infinite Soul Spiritual development centre in Narellan, NSW.

For more information go to www.infinitesoul.com.au or www.amandaroussety.com

Children and Healing with Angels

Artwork credit: Heilige Schutzengel / Guardian Angel – Print by Lindberg

There is nothing quite so special as the connection Children can have with Angels Nathan Ho explains.

Children have an innate and natural connection to their intuition and their Divine Guidance. They have a level of innocence that brings about a sense of clarity without judgment. This is usually being more connected to the imagination, which is in fact, the interpreter of messages and signs from the Universe. As a Clairvoyant Healer and Teacher, I have had the privilege and the honour of working with children in fun, dynamic and exciting ways to teach them about what is really a natural and inborn connection to themselves, the world within them and the world all around them.

One of the most prominent ways that I have worked with Children is through facilitating experiential and hands on workshops for them and their parents, all with the intention of developing a better understanding about themselves and the loving and benevolent presence of the Angelic Kingdom in their everyday lives. What I find most empowering about these workshops is the level of shared understanding that develops between a child and their parent/s as a result of the experience.

For instance, a parent may be concerned about what their child is experiencing, be that what they hear, see, feel or think, and this might not be considered 'normal' amongst their peers. When parents hear about these workshops and they come along to see what these connections are all about, both the children and parents develop a better understanding and awareness of these experiences. Resulting from this, they are able to feel more comfortable about their spiritual gifts; working with them to support their lives, rather than rejecting them and living in fear of themselves and what they can accomplish with Divine Intervention or Spiritual Assistance.

Children love Angels! They can feel the love and the support that they radiate, and in knowing that they call upon their Angels for all sorts of things, I have seen children of all different backgrounds and ability levels shine in a whole different way. This brings a warm feeling to my heart, knowing that the blessings that have come about resulting from Angelic connections can be spread and shared to other family members and friends. Reflecting upon this however, it also reminds me that connecting with Angels in everyday life is simple and needn't be complicated.

Whilst in previous generations, to be spiritually open to Angels would have many thinking some of the following things:

- They would need to be from a certain religious background,
- They would be possibly be seen as out of the ordinary, or
- Having these spiritual and intuitive connections would mean that they would need to be doing healings and readings as their 'profession'.

Working with children and teaching them to develop their awareness and relationships with the Angelic Kingdom has, however, demonstrated something much more profound. Because these connections can be so easily established and maintained, and as we are moving towards a more accepting and open-minded world, we need to also understand that being a healer means much more than healing for the purpose of healing others and seeing clients. Whilst that is one aspect of it, it also builds upon the principles of being a healer in every walk of life. Working with Children and teaching them to connect with their Angels has demonstrated that different people, regardless of their age, background, culture, religion and life experience, all have the ability to connect with and heal with the Angels. In order to be the healer it involves one to do the self-healing and to be able to hold the light in all different expressions and representations of life.

Healing can also involve other things such as,

- Cheering up an upset person,
- Helping out other children and adults in need,
- Being able to listen to others who need to share,
- Forgiving others,
- Loving unconditionally, and
- Finding the best in other people, places and situations.

Working with the Angelic Kingdom has taught me that Angels love each of us unconditionally and that there is an Angel inside each and every one of us. Through sharing this message onto the children of today and tomorrow, I intend to remind them of the great light inside of them, just like how a candle lights the wick of other candles. To enlighten, inspire, educate and spread a message of peace, one person at a time.

Blessings and love,

Nathan and Friends

Nathan Star combines his experiences, passions and talents as an ANGEL THERAPIST®, Clairvoyant Healer and Primary School Teacher to offer a unique approach to healing and teaching adults and children of all ages. For more information about Nathan or the work that he does, please visit his website at www.nathanstar.com

A Little Healing Goes A Long Way.

By Sue Bishop

An extract from Secrets of the Soul by Sue Bishop

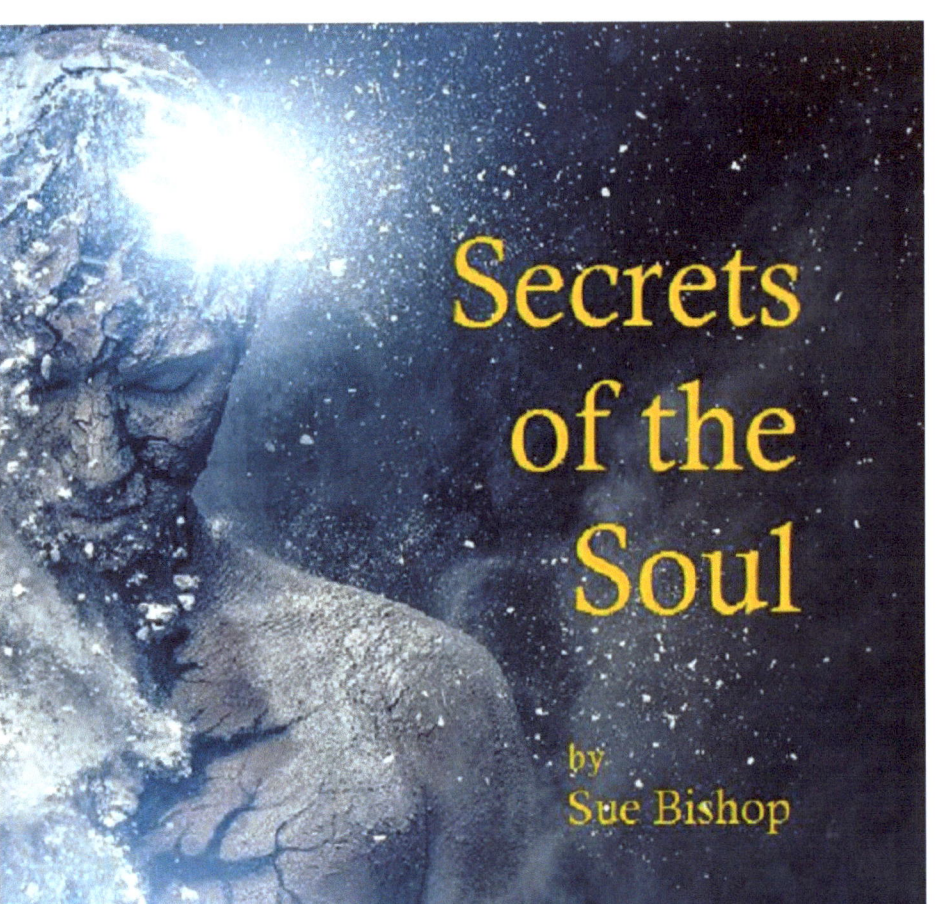

Sue Bishop is one of Australia's top psychic intuitive and author of 'Sixth Sense' and 'Psychic Kids' (Allen&Unwin). Sue is also the Director of The Chiara College of Metaphysics that specialises in psychic, spiritual and personal development. She has appeared on the Morning Show and on radio.

To contact Sue please visit: *http://www.chiaracollege.com.au*

Chakra and auric healing are labels that tend to suggest a fantastic notion of energy healing to the uninitiated - all outstretched arms and incantations - when in reality they are well-ordered systems created to explore and work with life energy, sometimes called 'prana' or 'qi'.

As a spiritual healer I work with these systems, channelling both universal and earth energy to rebalance the chakras and the aura. I manipulate energy and check the condition of each chakra and how it is connected to my client's physical, mental, emotional and spiritual states.

Through this process you can literally be re-charged. Energy starts to move and release old problems or feelings that you may have locked away for months, even years.

The role of a spiritual or psychic healer is to help people understand themselves, to help them find the strengths and weaknesses reflected in the physical body, and this in turn ties in perfectly with their whole spiritual journey. Spiritual healing is energetic healing. It's a modality which removes the blockages or restrictions that prevent us from accessing and becoming our true selves.

From a metaphysical perspective, blocked energy creates illness. When we are at 'dis-ease' with ourselves and we fail to do anything about the situation, eventually the physical body becomes ill or suffers from disease. Illness is not the cause of our problems but the end result of our spiritual malaise. It is the soul's way of telling us to stop, look and listen to the inner self and to make changes in our life. Each energy block is associated with a spiritual lesson. So, when you unblock the energy, there will be an associated awareness. That's when things start to go deeper - as the client talks and understands, they release energy and that in turn is reflected in the chakra system.

You can learn to 'energetically' heal yourself. How? Start by looking at why the heart and heart on the same page.

Look at your body. How many times has it slipped into illness because of a belief system that has been in conflict with the desire of the soul? What is the underlying karmic pattern that keeps cropping up in your life? Think about it for a moment.

Why do you have a predisposition to certain ailments?

What lessons are you meant to learn from these ailments?

What soul lesson are you choosing to ignore?

When you get sick, stop and think about what your body is saying. What part of your body is being affected?

A simple way of recognising where the spiritual problem lies is to pinpoint the part of your body affected and relate it to a restrictive belief associated with the chakra consciousness that governs that region of your body.

• Problems in your legs, feet, bones, lower back, anus, sexual organs and large intestine indicate base chakra issues.

• Problems with the circulatory system, the kidneys, bladder, womb and reproductive organs are associated with sacral chakra issues.

• Problems with the digestive system, stomach, pancreas, liver, spleen, pancreas, gall bladder, lumbar vertebrae and muscles indicate solar plexus issues

• Problems in the thymus gland and in the heart and lung region and arms are associated with heart chakra issues.

• Problems in the throat area, in the larynx, upper shoulders, mouth and jaw reflect throat chakra issues.

• Problems with the spinal cord, eyes, ears, nose and sinuses are related to the third eye chakra.

• Problems with the cerebral cortex and the central nervous system indicate crown chakra issues.

Knowing these connections helps us understand the consciousness behind our illness, why our bodies get sick, but there are other things we have to be aware of. Some physical conditions can reflect issues relating to several chakras at the same time. And in some cases, pain in one area can have causes elsewhere. We can also create some of our illness and disease by exercising our free will. By this I mean we might inadvertently be living in an environmentally toxic suburb or we might choose to eat the wrong foods and not exercise or ignore all of our body's warning signs. Even when we fall sick due to our own actions, the part of the body affected will still reflect underlying beliefs or chakra issues.

That's why two people might smoke the same amount and one of them gets throat cancer while the other doesn't. If you examine the life of the person with throat cancer it is more than likely you'll find long-term unresolved throat chakra issues. This by no means suggests they consciously want to get cancer, even though smoking is obviously dangerous and contributes to the disease, but the spiritual cause lies in throat chakra issues.

The other thing to be aware of is that some illnesses and diseases are the direct result of pre-birth karma. A karmic illness or disease should never be misconstrued to imply that you are being punished for misdemeanours from a previous life. No karmic illness is punishment. It is just an opportunity for growth. A karmic disease may be programmed into the DNA to erupt at a particular point in our lives to draw our attention to certain issues we need to learn in order to facilitate further spiritual growth.

Karmic influences precipitate certain specific tendencies toward illness by creating predominant patterns known as miasms. They can increasingly weaken the physical body's resistance to illness and facilitate the manifestation of disease. A miasm, which represents the karmic potential for disease, usually lies dormant within the subtle bodies of the human aura. It is activated by the soul to draw conscious awareness to whatever area of life requires immediate attention. When a miasm is activated, its ethereal template is projected via the subtle bodies through the bio magnetic field. It first appears at a molecular level before moving into the physical body.

It is also possible for a karmic illness or disease to develop at a particular stage in someone's life not only for their growth, but also for the spiritual growth of their family members or friends.

If the soul decided before incarnating that the lesson should result in the death of the physical body by cancer, the death will occur from this disease. However, should the soul decide on a different karmic path, where cancer doesn't cause death, then getting cancer is just a consequence of the lesson, rather than the point of the lesson.

To heal ourselves we need to recognise underlying spiritual imbalances and then set about restoring harmony and balance to our energy system. I know this concept might be new to some people, that it doesn't fit into the allopathic (traditional) healing model, but by broadening our understanding of healing to include concepts such as removing blocked energy and resolving restrictive issues from our chakras and aura we can make a world of difference to our general well being. Traditional medicine is fantastic for healing such things as broken bones and for getting immediate relief from pain or physical body crisis, but if we add to this the healing of the emotional, mental and spiritual problems, there's no need for the illness or disease to return again and again.

I know a woman who healed herself of terminal breast cancer after western medicine gave up on her. When I asked her, 'How did you do it?' she said, 'With the power of my mind. I'm a single mother with three children. I couldn't afford to die and leave them alone so I willed myself better.' Obviously her disease was not based on pre-birth karma and she had a very strong mind. She believed she could get better and she manifested that reality.

Healing is an opportunity to learn about ourselves. It is the soul's way of getting us to pay attention to what we are doing and where we are going. Next time you fall ill think about nurturing yourself on all levels.

A Blessing in Disguise

How Whooping Cough Kicked My Butt
& Brought Me Back to Myself with Meadow Linn

You're probably familiar with the expression "A blessing in disguise". However, sometimes that blessing is so well disguised that no matter how hard you look, all you can see is the anguish that's ripping at your heart and shredding you into tiny pieces. This might sound a bit dramatic, but that's truly how it can feel when you're mired in a difficult situation.

Have you ever been so frustrated by your inability to be a party to your own life that you had moments where you found yourself pleading with God for it all to be over? That's what my journey with whooping cough was like. Although many days during my two-month convalescence were passed contentedly watching TV, there were other days when quelling my tears of frustration took every ounce of energy I could muster.

The most difficult time wasn't when I felt the worst, because during those weeks I didn't have the energy to care. It wasn't until I was starting to heal that I was aware of how hard it was to have no income and no social interactions. However, this is also when I realized that there had to be a reason, some sort of blessing in disguise.

The months I spent in bed were during the time period I'd originally set aside to jumpstart my career. But when you barely have the energy to feed yourself, spending time figuring out your Life Plan is not exactly top of the to-do list. So, I had to let go. I had to go with the flow and allow my body the time it needed to heal.

I began to see this journey as a chrysalis phase, leading to an eventual metamorphosis. I pictured myself cocooned by my surroundings. And when the time was right, when my energy returned, I would soar like a butterfly. I fully believed this, and this helped me through the rough days.

The problem was - when I finally felt better, there were bills to pay, articles to write, e-mails to return, and home repairs to do. Nothing felt different. If anything, life felt ho-hum and tedious because there was so much catching up to do.

How could I have made it through such a trying time and feel no different? What was the point? Of course, germs were the reason I was sick. But, wasn't there a greater reason, something that made it all worth it? Where was my blessing in disguise?

Gravely disappointed, my heart ached. I was lonely, way behind on work, and as of yet, I couldn't see any type of personal or professional metamorphosis taking place. My voice shaking, I lamented this to my mom while gasping for air between sobs.

My mom reminded me that even after the butterfly emerges from its chrysalis, it doesn't immediately fly off to sip a flower's sweet nectar. Before it spreads its beautiful wings, it first hangs on the branch and waits. The metamorphosis isn't complete the moment the butterfly breaks through its shell. There's a waiting period, while it adjusts to its new surroundings and its newfound identity.

My life hasn't changed dramatically since my illness; however, once I understood that I needed to be patient, the urgency for transformation was gone and I was able to relax. Once that happened, amazing opportunities began to fall into my lap.

Of course, I wish I hadn't gotten sick, but I am now able to see the blessing in disguise. Had I been vigorously seeking my life plan, I wouldn't have been in the right frame of mind to simply accept the blessings of the Universe. I would have been struggling to attain something, whereas now I feel like I've planted seeds that with gentle care and nurturing will eventually grow strong and vibrant. It will all unfold in due time.

Life throws us curve balls. And although it may not seem like it today, tomorrow, or maybe even a few years from now, eventually you will understand what your challenging experiences taught you and discover the blessing in disguise. Here's to being patient! Here's to keeping on keeping on, even when it feels like you're heading nowhere. Good things are coming your way.

Green Eggs and Tomatoes - A Healing Breakfast

When healing from physical or emotional challenges, it's valuable to have a healthy and delicious breakfast to set the tone for the day. The greens and tomatoes will make you feel light and free, but the protein in the eggs will give you the necessary sustenance to carry on with strength and determination.

Serves 1
2 tsp. olive oil, divided
½ cup grape tomatoes (the smaller the better)
2 large handfuls of Power Greens (baby spinach, baby chard, and baby kale)
2 free-range or pastured eggs
Fresh cracked pepper and artisanal sea salt (optional)

Warm 1 tsp. of olive oil in a nonstick pan or well-seasoned cast iron pan over medium heat. Add the tomatoes and cook for one or two minutes, until just soft. Add the greens and briefly sauté until wilted. Remove from pan and put on a plate. Add the remaining 1 tsp. of olive oil to the pan and fry the eggs to your liking. Place the egg on top of the greens and sprinkle with salt and pepper. Enjoy with gusto!

Meadow Linn is a writer and a chef, living in California with her dog, cats and chicken. She believes that living well and eating well should be tasty and fun. Meadow has just co-authored her first cookbook with Denise Linn which is available now through Amazon. **Contact Meadow at**: www.meadowlinn.com and www.savortheday.com

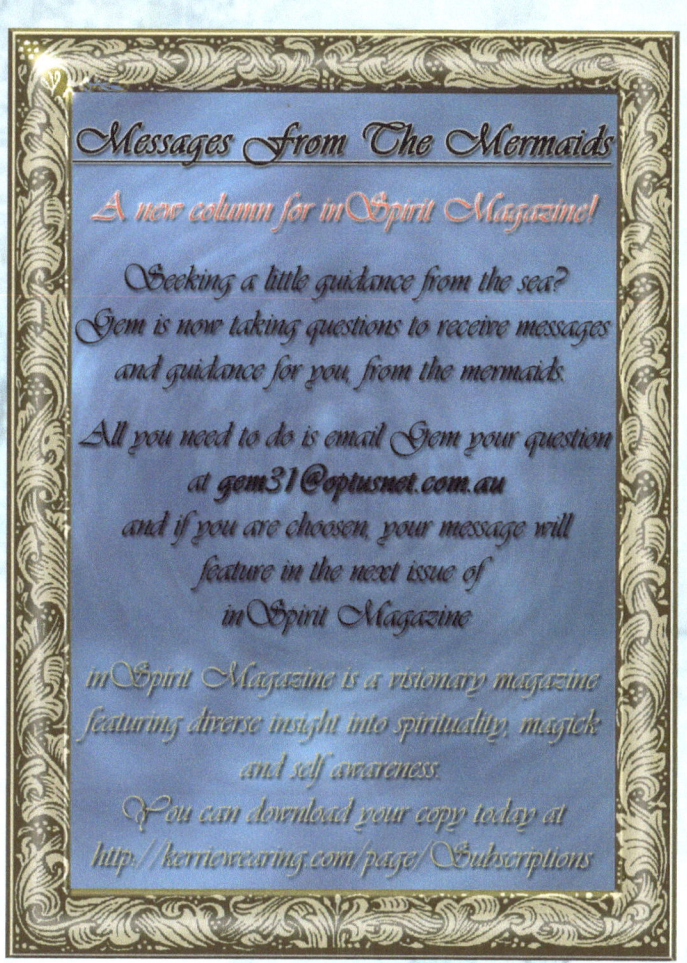

SUBSCRIBE NOW

InSpirit

Annual digital subscriptions available for just

$7.95AUD

www.inspiritmagazine.com

Playful Healing

Rita Maher explores the playful ways you can engage children to uncover healing and awareness.

> As children we look to the adults and peers that surround us for a sense of self.

All of us have times in our life when we are hurt, wounded, left with erroneous beliefs about who we are. Children are no different; in fact children tend to hold on tighter in some cases to the hurt and wounds and they carry into later life the erroneous beliefs that were inflicted upon them at a younger age.

As children we look to the adults and peers that surround us for a sense of self. They help shape who we are to become as we grow and develop. Most of the time children grow without incident, and have no problem adjusting to the world that surrounds them, taking their place in life and making it their own. But what happens to the child that struggles, to the child that hears a negative and takes it to heart, to the child who is unsure of their place? How do we help the children that, for whatever reason, are finding it hard to deal with the world around them and how to make sense of it all?

Helping our children adjust to life and find their way is one the greatest gifts we have, and can also be a great challenge to parents. Are we getting it right? What if we say the wrong thing? Am I too strict or too lenient? All questions that cause parents to self-doubt at times the best way to help their children develop - after all they did not arrive with an instruction guide, and we know how to do what we do from what we learnt and observed growing

up. Introducing playful methods can help in the healing of children.

Recently I went and explored one playful way of helping children understand how they feel and why they feel the way they do. I visited Counsellor and Sandplay Therapist Kerryn Armor, who is located in Sydney's south western suburbs, for a Sandplay session. Kerryn has been working with children for many years and included Sandplay in her practice, which she says is not only for children but can benefit adults as well. Stepping into her rooms it felt like I was walking back into childhood - toys, figurines, props, pictures adorn all the walls of the room. In one corner is a trolley which holds a plastic container full of sand. Kerryn's approach is relaxed and comfortable. She asks if there is anything I wish to discuss, and then allows me to just talk. After a period of time she brings the trolley with the sand in over, and says "Simply place your hands in it, feel it, shape it, create whatever patterns you want in it." This is called charging the sand, she explains later, and allows you to become relaxed with the process. She then explains that I can place whatever I want in the sand. As I scan the room, there are literally hundreds of items I can choose from, so I take my time and select those that I feel represent me and my story for that day.

Kerryn explains that this method of placing objects in the sand helps to tell the story and the emotions that we sometimes don't want to talk about, each area of the sand representing different aspects of our life. From how we place the objects and how we then explain them to Kerryn, she is able to build a bigger picture of what is going on for us, and uses this knowledge to help people move forward and heal, adjust, and empower them in life. Sandplay therapy is unobtrusive and it feels natural to play in the sand. It allows for you to get lost in your story and allow true untapped pictures, emotions and feelings to emerge. This is a therapy I would recommend for children as it allows them to just play and be themselves. By doing so it allows their story to be revealed and presents a perfect opportunity for help to be given.

Another playful way is the use of drawing and cards to help children understand their emotions and explore ways of dealing with these emotions. Children, like us, need to understand that we will not always be happy. Sometimes we can feel sad, we can be angry, or confused. Children make mistakes and that's ok as well. The great news is we can move forward and turn these feelings around and learn to deal with them in a positive way. We can also teach our children to set positive tones for the day with the use of affirmation cards. They can pull a card out and hold that thought in their mind as they move through the day. 'Happy Little Minds' is a set of affirmation cards that I have designed as a holistic and intuitive counsellor. The inspiration for these cards is my own children, one of whom struggles with his learning and how to fit in at times in life. By designing these cards, I found it was important for him to be able to just grab a card and to tell me how he feels. We then had an opportunity to sit and talk through the emotion. Sometimes children just don't want to tell you what's going on, or they just don't know the words to use. The cards' illustrations allow children to connect with the picture to explain the emotion and give tools on how to work through it. Children can even design their own affirmation card.

Which brings me to another playful way to help your child. Drawing or art are great ways to help your child explore their emotions without having to sit there and feel like they need to explain everything to you. I am sure you have at some time experienced it yourself - not wanting to explain how you feel, just wanting to feel better or happy instead, but unsure how to do so. Grab a scrap book, coloured pencils and let your children draw how they feel. After they have drawn the picture you can sit and talk to them about it. Ask them to draw how they want to feel. Sometimes the drawing process itself can help change the mood or child's perception, and help shift the hurt. This is a tool I use in my counselling services with children.

Finally, a great way to change a negative emotion to a positive emotion is to exercise, so get outside and play. Kick a ball around with your child and watch them smile and laugh as they release anger and frustration. Go for a run in the park or a bike ride, roll down a hill and just enjoy some time together. A big warm hug at the end will help as well.

So be playful and help heal any hurts, wounds or erroneous beliefs so that your child can feel safe and secure and happy as they move through life.

Rita Maher is a Psychic Medium, Intuitive Counsellor and qualified Reiki Healer who has a passion for working with children and families. She specialises in meditation and intuitive guidance to help not just children but adults understand direction and change in their life, helping create secure environments for young minds to grow and thrive.

You can book a Sandplay therapy by contacting Kerryn Armor on 0475 193 960 or you book a holistic counselling session with Rita Maher by visiting www.ritamaher.com or contact her on 0434 867 426 Happy Little Minds can be purchased from Rita's site as well.

Shell Vibrations

Gem Green, our Goddess of the Sea unveils the healing essence of the Ocean and her Shells here, for you to add to your healing tool kit.

Since the dawn of time the ocean has been a natural place of healing. She has the power to ease your emotions, to calm your inner storms, to release your pain and anguish and to restore balance within your spiritual essence. Simply being in her presence, smelling her salty breath, feeling the kiss of her winds on your face, hearing her reassuring tones as waves fall onto the shore, touching her magickal waters with your toes or seeing her in all her glory, is enough to feel the powerful effects of her healing embrace.

So amazing is this healing wonder that every little aspect to ocean has an energetic vibration seemingly tailor-made for what your heart and soul requires. Each shell, each speck of sand, each piece of seaweed, every drop of water, each and every animal, microscopic or large, is healing to your spirit, your soul.

The benefits of connecting with oceanic energies for healing are as immense as they are diverse for the body, mind and soul, yet oceanic energies harbour a seemingly insatiable focus on the emotional, spiritual and soul levels to encourage living within the divine realms of your authentic spirit.

My connections on the healing aspects, energies or vibrations of ocean and seas is a beautiful, transformative, complicated, and at times tough, work in progress that I am passionate about and treasure deeply. Seashells have been at the forefront of my passion and I am drawn to sharing with you a little more knowledge on the healing vibrations of some amazing bones of the sea.

Powerful tools for healing, the use of seashells is very beneficial as they emit a vibrational energy for connections and healings. Each shell has its own unique energy to impart, each family or class of shell has a group energy, and each species has unique energy too. Example: Clam shells represent abundance, communication, foundations and grounding. The Venus Clam shell can add a connection to the goddess Venus, beauty and the cosmic universe. The unique Venus Clam shell YOU are using will add a unique and personal element pertinent to your journey or that of the healing recipient.

We are blessed to be able to utilise the healing energy of seashells in a number of ways and these include meditation and visualisation, healing altars, seashell waters, wearing them in the form of jewellery and the laying of shells upon or around the physical body.

Quick Guide

Use your intuitive senses, your imagination and your guides, feel the energy, see the energy, healing and balancing, penetrating deeply in whatever form you have chosen to use it.

Mactra Shell - The essence of the Mactra shell brings in a powerful energy for boring deep and boring fast, allowing its vibrational energy to delve deeply and quickly. The Mactra shell is very good at revealing the root of issues and offers immediate relief. The Mactra shell is also beneficial with mental health issues, health, happiness and wellbeing in general.

Heart Cockle Shell - The essence of the Heart Cockle shell surrounds and embraces love. These shells are great for heart healing, general calmness and centring.

Oyster Shells - The essence of the Oyster shell provides stability and longevity and these shells are great for balance and mental health. The more purple the Oyster Shell, the more in sync with Third Eye chakra healing as well.

Scallop Shell - The essence of the Scallop shell offers an amazing peaceful quality and creates balance, harmony and happiness. The Scallop shells encourage movement and create joy.

Clam Shell - The essence of the Clam shell provides an energy to enhance communication and foundations as well as healing, stability and vitality. They also assist in creating balance and happiness within one's self.

Sea Urchin Shell - The Sea Urchin shell represents many different aspects in life situations and can create relief from temple based headaches and aches connected to the eyes. The Sea Urchin shell aids recovery in general.

Abalone Shell - The essence of the Abalone shell centres around the heart and beauty, providing a divine healing energy for the heart and issues surrounding inner beauty and acceptance. The Abalone shell also assists with the ears, hearing and listening, insight and foresight, releasing trauma and returning one "home" (physically and spiritually). The Abalone nourishes and nurtures very well.

Cowrie Shell – The essence of the Cowrie shell is essentially all things feminine and they can provide healing energies for many female health issues, especially around reproduction and the inner workings of the female body. The Cowrie is beneficial in soul healings, balancing out karmic debt and past life regression.

Gem embraces the energetic power of seashells, sea animals and the waters of ocean and sea every day, connecting and creating with this amazing and unique energy to enhance and guide not only her magickal life journey but yours as well if you allow it. "May The Magick & Wisdom of Ocean & Sea's Inspire Us All" www.gemgreen.com.au

AVAILABLE NOW
FOR DELIVERY IN NOV

Palmistry is an intuitive art and a highly accurate tool which gives you much insight about others and of course yourself.

Max Coppa's newest book, Love between the Lines will provide you with the tools to find your own answers, assist you to recognise the signs and ultimately control the destiny of your love life.

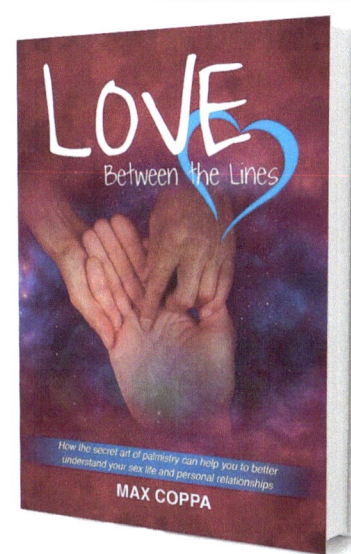

www.inspiritpublishing.net

Advertise with Us

Advertise with inSpirit Magazine for :

- Best price value advertising,
- Your targeted market
- Cross promotion with Facebook and our email database

Contact us today at email: mail@inspiritpublishing.net

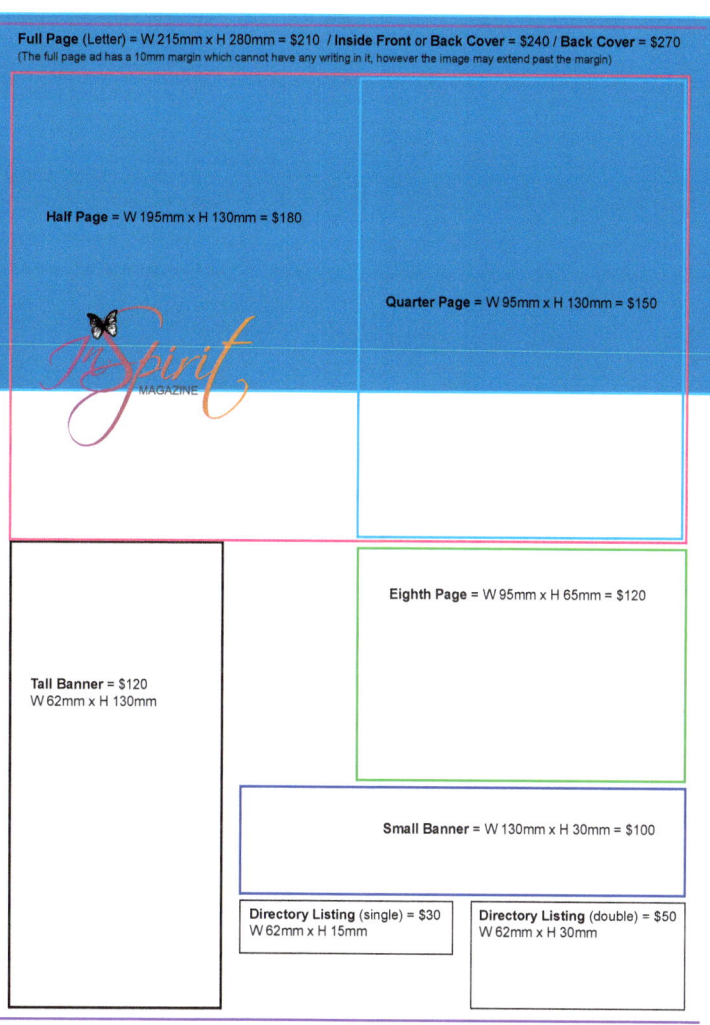

inSPIRIT | Directory

AUTHORS

SERENE CONNEELEY
BLESSED BEE
www.SereneConneeley.com

JUDE DOWNES
FROM GRIEF TO GODDESS
www.fromgrieftogoddess.com

ARTWORK

NICOLLE POLL
Artwork by Nicolle - Oracle Cards, Animal Magick Series, Soul Journey Portraits
E: artworkbynicolle@bigpond.com
FB: www.facebook.com/ArtworkByNicolle

NICOLA MCINTOSH
Graphic Design, Fairy & Fantasy Art, Oracle Cards & Writer
www.nicolamcintosh.com

ASTROLOGERS

DAVID WELLS
Teacher, Qabalist, Astrologer, Author & Past Life Therapist
www.davidwells.co.uk

CRYSTAL SHOPS

JOPO FENG SHUI & CRYSTALS
2 Revesby Road, Revesby NSW
T: +612 9785 0798

SPIRIT STONE
For crystals & new age supplies
www.spiritstone.com.au

MAGICAL TOOLS

NATASHA HEARD
Blessed Branches
www.blessedbranches.com

GEM GREEN
Ocean and Sea Weaving
www.gemgreen.com.au

NUMEROLOGY

AMANDA COPPA
Crystal Healer, Numerology & Astrology
www.facebook.com/cosmiccodes

PALMISTRY

MAX COPPA
Palmistry and Numerology
www.maxcoppa.com

PAST LIVES

TONI REILLY
Past Life Regress, Intutive Counselling
www.tonireilly.com.au

PERSONAL GROWTH

KYE CROW
Wunjo Crow – Sacred Clothing, Animal Sanctuary & Sacred Journey into the Animal Realm workshops
www.camelcampsanctuary.com
www.facebook.com/Wunjocrow

Would you like your listing included here? Email us at
mail@inspiritpublishing.net for details.

PSYCHICS & MEDIUMS

KERRIE WEARING
Author, Soul Coach & Medium
www.psychicmedium.com.au

RITA MAHER
Psychic Medium, Intuitive Counsellor and qualified Reiki Healer
www.steppingstones4life.com

AMANDA ROUSSETY
Psychic Medium and Infinite Soul Development Center
www.amandaroussety.com

SHAMANISM

LAURA NAOMI
Consultations, Workshops & Seminars
www.laura-naomi.com

STORYTELLING & FOLKLORE

REILLY McCARRON
Faerie Bard, Folklorist & Storyteller with Harp
www.faeriebard.com
E: info@faeriebard.com
F: Faerie Bard

RADIO SHOWS

www.ghostsofoz.com

inSPIRIT | review

Reviews by Rita Maher and Nicolle Poll

CONVERSATIONS WITH MEDIUMS

Author: Scott Podmore
Published: Balboa Press

Take a journey into the unknown, the unseen, the area of belief and scepticism in Scott Podmore's book Conversations with Mediums.

For those who have ever wondered how they do that, what they see, why they do that, and what it means to them to be a medium, this book is for you. No need to keep wondering why; simply share in the conversations between Scott and 12 mediums. A journey that took 2 years and allowed Scott to interview over 30 mediums, allowing him to ask the hard question and delve deeper to bring to light a greater understanding of the mediums' world.

The conversations with mediums, 12 of which are captured in this book, ask you to open your mind to new possibilities. This book reads itself effortlessly to you; you are there having the conversation, and as it flowed I found myself pondering the same questions that Scott was asking. Entwined in the dialogue there were a few surprises along the way that had me pausing to take in what I had read before moving on. It matters not if you believe or not, nor what your understanding is of the medium's world at this stage, by reading this book you are sure to step back and ask question of yourself and expand your views, or form new understandings of the way mediumship works.

A well written book that left me wanting to hear more.

SEVEN SACRED SITES

Author: Serene Conneeley
Published: Blessed Bee Publishing

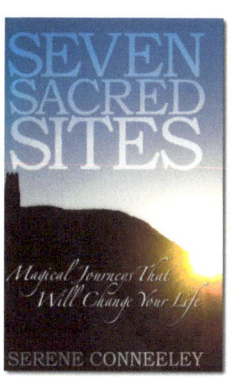

Serene Conneeley's book Seven Sacred Sites is a powerhouse of memories, ancient knowledge and wisdom, and will take you on a personal journey of discovery.

As you turn through each page in this magical book, Serene paints the landscape as only she can; her pen is the artist's paintbrush and her words are the scholars of ancient times' teaching.

As you take a journey around the world exploring Machu Picchu in Peru, monuments of ancient Egypt, Stonehenge, The Camino in Northern Spain, Hawaii, Avalon in England and Uluru in Australia, your soul will refuel itself and leave you wanting to journey there in person. Each site you visit imparts its wisdom, ancient knowledge and traditions upon you. I found myself being drawn back in time, back to truth and beauty when I read this book. From the moment I picked it up my travel plans for the future expanded as I yearned to step foot on the sacred ground.

If you are travelling to any of these areas this book is a must, but even if not, this book is perfect for anyone wishing to gain the understanding of forgotten culture and traditions. The history included in the book gives credit to Serene's meticulous attention to detail, and allows the reader to immerse themselves fully.

Beautiful seems too simple a word to describe this book, yet it describes perfectly all that Serene captures and conveys to the reader as they journey with their mind, body and soul to seven Sacred Sites.

THE CRYSTAL GRID ORACLE

Author: Nicola McIntosh
Published: Self Published with Spirit Stone /www.spiritstone.com.au

Nicola McIntosh has created a series of 36 visually stunning Crystal Grid cards, with a beautiful Limited Edition additional card, that are energetically strong, with all the cards giving the feel of flow and connectedness.

The Crystal Grid combinations remind me of the magick of snowflakes with their beauty and with no two patterns ever the same, all the cards presenting as symbolic and varied.

The Guide Book is easy to understand and navigate, the card size easy to shuffle. I initially drew a three card spread, asking what I needed to know the most and I received an extremely accurate reading. This continued with further variations of card spreads used. I love the energy I felt zinging from these cards, how easy they are to connect to, and the honesty and accuracy of information received when working with them.

The Crystal Grid Oracle enhances the user's knowledge about crystals and how crystal grids work, adding a unique and powerful connective tool to your collection.

Volume 8 Issue 1
The Healing Issue
www.inspiritmagazine.com